MEN-AT-ARMS SERIES

EDITOR: MARTIN WINDROW

Rome's Enemies:
Germanics and Dacians

Text by PETER WILCOX

Colour plates by G. A. EMBLETON

OSPREY PUBLISHING LONDON

Published in 1982 by
Osprey Publishing Ltd
Member company of the George Philip Group
12–14 Long Acre, London WC2E 9LP
© Copyright 1982 Osprey Publishing Ltd

Reprinted 1984, 1985, 1986, 1987 (twice), 1988

British Library Cataloguing in Publication Data

Wilcox, Peter
    Rome's enemies. — (Men-at-arms series; 129)
    1. Barbarian invasions of Rome
    2. Germanic tribes   2. Dacians
    I. Title   II. Series
    937′.09   DG504

    ISBN 0-85045-473-5

Filmset in Great Britain
Printed in Hong Kong

Author's Note:
This book does not pretend to original scholarship.
With certain exceptions, such as line artwork, it was
compiled from secondary sources. Its purpose is to
give a general survey of the German and Dacian
warriors who fought against the forces of Rome.

Chronology

See Glossary of terms and names on page 38.

3000 B.C. Indo-Europeans spread into north-west Europe, where they settle among earlier populations of Neolithic farmers and Old Stone-Age hunters.

2000 B.C. Celto-Ligurian tribes are in control of large areas of central and western Europe. Represented by the 'Bell-Beaker Folk', they begin moving into the British Isles. Other Indo-Europeans move east, where the Thracians and Iranians form two large groups. The Balts and Slavs occupy most of what is now Germany. Illyrian tribes occupy an area of southern Europe between the Italian peninsula and Greece. (Italic Indo-Europeans had moved into their peninsula, and warlike Greek tribes into the Mediterranean area, from the Danube region.)

The Teutons of this period are in possession of most of the Scandinavian peninsula, where a racially distinct Germanic Nordic has developed from a mixture of invading Indo-European Nordics and Old Stone-Age survivors. Indo-European tribes now possess most of Europe at the expense of the earlier stock who are now either pushed into the more inaccessible parts of the continent, or become the lower strata of society, the untouchables of Europe.

Germans, from Trajan's Column, dedicated in 113 A.D.; their impressive physique is clearly illustrated. One sports the Suebian hair-knot. Two cloak styles are evident: one is large, folded double, with a thick fringe of tassels, while the other (top right) is a circular type with a diagonal head-opening.

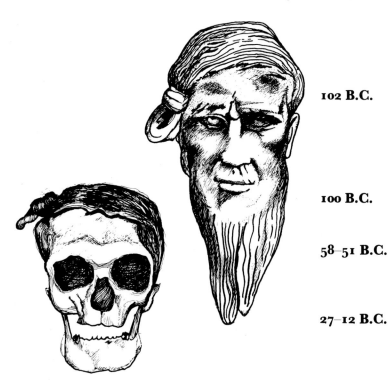

The skull of an old man, 1st century A.D., found at Eckenn-ford, Schleswig-Holstein; the reddish blonde hair is combed and twisted into a neat Suebian knot. Compare this with the carved head of a German chieftain, possibly of one of the Danubian tribes, from the tomb of A. Julius Pompilius, one of Marcus Aurelius's generals, 175 A.D. (National Museum, Terme)

600 B.C. The continental Celts begin the Halstatt phase of their magnificent Iron Age culture; at about this time they over-run central Spain.

400 B.C. The second phase of Celtic Iron Age culture evolves; known as the La Tène, it represents the flowering of Celtic abstract art, seen, *inter alia*, in the decoration of weapons. Halstatt Celts move into Britain.

La Tène Celts cross the Alps and take control of northern Italy. Etruscan colonies in the Po valley are obliterated, and Rome is sacked during a protracted Celtic raid down the peninsula.

350 B.C. Rome defeats the Celts in Italy.
300 B.C. Rome gains full control of Italy.
115 B.C. Celtic tribes from the middle Danube area, the Cimbri and Teutones invade Gaul; during the extensive raid they attract the Ambrones—another Celtic tribe—to their ranks, and destroy five Roman armies sent against them before turning towards Italy.

102 B.C. The Cimbri, Teutones and Ambrones are annihilated by the new model Roman army, which had been created, trained and was now led to victory by Marius, a General of obscure background.

100 B.C. The Goths cross the Baltic from the Scandinavian peninsula to northern Germany.

58–51 B.C. Julius Caesar conquers most of the Celtic tribes of Gaul and reportedly repulses an attempted invasion by trans-Rhenian tribes.

27–12 B.C. Roman forces advance in central and eastern Europe, to the Danube; the river thus forms, for most of its length, the northern frontier of the Empire. The expansion of the Frontier to the Elbe in the north is called off after the disaster in the Teutoburg Forest. At about this time Augustus creates a standing army of 25 legions.

A.D. 9. The garrison of northern Germany, consisting of the XVII, XVIII and XIX Legions are wiped out in an ambush in the Teutoburg Forest. These three legions never again appeared on the army list. The Rhine-Danube nexus now marks the northern limits of the Roman Empire.

A.D. 43. Roman forces invade Britain, speedily overrunning a third of the country, from the southern coast.

A.D. 69–79. The angle formed by the Rhine and Danube is rounded off. Roman occupation of the British lowlands is carried up to the highlands. A further two legions are lost during a revolt of auxiliaries on the Rhine.

A.D.81. Several campaigns are mounted by the Roman army on the Danube, particularly against the Thracian kingdom of Dacia.

A.D. 101.	The Emperor Trajan begins a massive invasion of Dacia; in two campaigns the Romans break Dacian resistance. The conquest creates a trans-Danubian salient of the Empire. Roman forces on the Danube are reinforced by four legions; Rhine legions are reduced by three.
A.D. 150.	Eastern German tribes begin drifting south; some of them enter into permanent federation.
A.D. 181.	A massive barbarian assault on the Danube provinces led by the Marcomanni and Quadi triggers off a prolonged series of savagely fought campaigns during the reign of the philosopher soldier Marcus Aurelius.
A.D. 251.	The Goths invade the Balkans and Anatolia; the Emperor Decius (Hostilianus) is killed.
A.D. 256.	Frankish and Alemannic war bands overrun Gaul and invade Spain and Italy.
A.D. 275.	Roman forces abandon both the Dacian salient and the Rhine-Danube angle in the face of increasing pressure along the northern frontier; the Gepids and Goths move into Dacia; the Alemanni occupy the Rhine-Danube angle and Burgundian tribes the middle Rhine area.
A.D. 280.	The Goths, led by their king Ermanarich, spread into a large area of Eurasia and north to the Baltic. 'Anglo-Saxon' raids increase on the east coast of Britain and northern coast of Gaul.
A.D. 358.	The Alemanni and Franks are defeated by the Emperor Julian in Gaul; some Franks remain in north-west Gaul as armed peasant marchmen (foederates), allies of Rome.
A.D. 360.	The Ostrogoths come into contact with westward-moving Huns, a Turco-Mongoloid people.
A.D. 372.	The Huns of the Volga attack the advancing Goths, who are overwhelmed by the nomadic hordes. The Huns are able to push into Europe, where they settle as the overlords of Slavonic peasants and Gepids on the Hungarian plains.
A.D. 375.	The Goths and Asding Vandals apply for sanctuary within the Empire. They are settled along the Danube, where they suffer many indignities at the hands of Roman merchants and officials.
A.D. 378.	The Visigoths are in revolt against Rome.
A.D. 379.	The Emperor of the East is killed, his army annihilated at Adrianople by the largely cavalry army of the Goths.
A.D. 380.	Germans, Sarmatians and Huns are taken into Imperial service; as a consequence, barbarian leaders begin to play an increasingly active rôle in the life of the Empire.

Reconstruction of cut of woollen twill tunic and trousers from Angeln, Denmark, dated to the 1st century B.C.

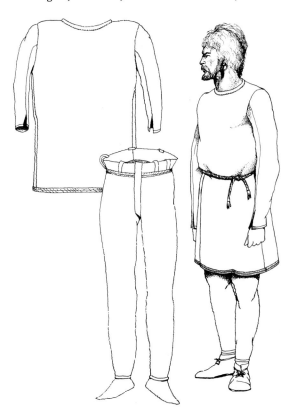

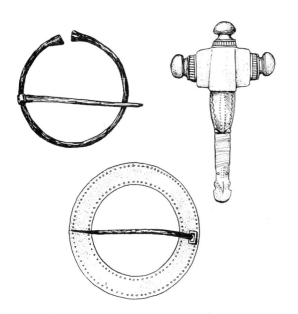

German cloak brooches.

A.D. 402. The Goths invade Italy, where they suffer defeat at the hands of the Romano-Vandal General Stilicho.

A.D. 405. Stilicho crushes a mixed army of Ostrogoths, Quadi and Asding Vandals with an army raised from the frontier forces of the Rhine, leaving this sector dangerously weakened.

A.D. 406. A coalition of Asding Vandals, Siling Vandals, Marcomanni, Quadi and a clan of Sarmatian Alans cross the frozen Rhine near Mainz into Gaul.

A.D. 407. Britain is denuded of the Roman garrison, which crosses the Channel in force in a sham effort to pacify the German invaders of Gaul. In fact they declare one of their number to be Emperor and seek recognition from the Franks, Burgundians and Alemanni who have occupied the left bank of the Rhine.

A.D. 409. The great barbarian coalition of Vandals, Suevi and Sarmatians which had ravaged Gaul for three years crosses the Pyrenees into Spain.

A.D. 410. Britain fragments under the local control of petty Romano-Celtic magnates. The Visigoths, led by Alaric, sack Rome.

A.D. 412. The Visigoths, in Imperial service, enter Gaul and depose yet another Imperial usurper.

A.D. 414. The Visigoths cross into Spain, where they exterminate the settled Siling Vandals and Sarmatian Alans (416). The Asding Vandals, Marcomanni and Quadi are spared, by Roman intervention, in order to prevent the increase of Visigothic power. As the reward for their exertions the Visigoths are invited by Roman authorities to settle in a large area of south-west Gaul.

A.D. 428. North Africa is invaded by the Asding Vandals; they build a pirate fleet and hold the Roman corn supply to ransom.

A.D. 433. Attila the Hun is born.

A.D. 436. The Huns drive deep into Germanic territory; many tribes become Hunnish vassals.

A.D. 449. German tribes begin the permanent settlement of Britain.

A.D. 451. Attila leads the Huns and their German vassals into Gaul; they are met and driven back by Roman troops, Burgundians, Salian Franks and Visigoths at the Campus Mauriacus. The Huns withdraw to Hungary.

A.D. 452. Attila invades Italy, but the Huns are bribed by Roman authorities to retire.

A.D. 453. Attila dies. The Vandals sack Rome.

A.D. 454. German vassals of the Huns overthrow their masters at the battle of Nedao.

A.D. 469-78. The Visigoths conquer most of Spain. The German general Odoacer becomes king of Italy and is recognised by the Eastern Roman Empire.

A.D. 493. Theodoric, king of the Ostrogoths, becomes Regent of Italy.

A.D. 507. The Franks expand into a large area of Gaul led by their king, Clovis.

A.D. 526. Theodoric dies.

A.D. 528. After defeating the Gepids the Lombards, helped by Avar nomads, invade Italy and make a permanent settlement in the north.

Introduction

In the report sent to his king from Acre in 1255 the Franciscan friar William of Rubruck, in reference to his travels in the Crimea, says: 'All the way from the Kherson to the mouth of the Tanais there are high mountain peaks along the coast, and there are forty villages between Kherson and Soldaia, of which almost every one has its own language. Dwelling here were many Goths, whose language is German . . .' Three centuries later, in about 1554, Augerois de Busbeck, a French traveller, came across a people he described as Goths on the shores of the Black Sea in the Crimea. After careful analysis of their language from examples surviving at the time of their discovery, philologists identified it as Gothic, with some alteration due to Slavonic influence. This people is now no longer traceable.

These chance references to all that remained of the once numerous and powerful Gothic nation cannot now be verified by the sophisticated anthropological methods available to us today. Thankfully, however, extensive skeletal evidence, not only of the Goths but of many other ancient Germanic peoples from the migration period, does exist. This fact has allowed anthropologists to establish the racial identity of peoples we would otherwise know by name only—colourless wraiths of the imagination.

During the thousand years before the Christian era two great Indo-European peoples, the Celts and Scythians, expanded into central and northern Europe—the Celts to the west, the Scyths to the east. They were followed by two more such groups—the Germans to the west, the Slavs to the east. Both the latter Indo-European groups were to have lasting effects on their chosen areas of

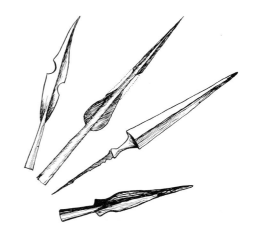

Celtic iron spearheads of the La Tène period.

settlement, and, later, throughout the planet— especially the Germans.

The period of Germanic migration, the Volkerwandurung, does not begin properly until the 3rd century. However, some see in the eventually abortive invasion of Roman Italy by a marauding Celtic horde the first southward probe involving Germanic warriors. These Cimbri and Teutones had destroyed several Roman armies in a series of encounters throughout Gaul between B.C. 114 and 102. The series of migrations did not end until the adoption of Christianity by the Norwegians in the 11th century A.D. Germanic homelands comprised modern Denmark, southern and central Norway, the north German coastal strip from the mouth of the Elbe to the Baltic shore, and the islands of Gotland and Bornholm. It was from these breeding grounds that warlike tribes, driven by pressures brought about by overpopulation, began their wanderings. Some have lost their names, being quickly absorbed into bigger Germanic groupings during the ensuing chaos. Populating the dank and gloomy forests of northern Europe, the German 'barbarians' who overran the western Empire were descendants of peasants who had taken up arms; at the time Tacitus wrote his *Germania* in the late 1st century A.D., a large proportion of the male population were warriors, tribal structure was in a state of flux, and their society was moving towards a crisis. Successful war leaders, normally elected

7

only for the duration of a single campaign, were becoming accepted in a permanent capacity as chieftains. The success of many leaders attracted other tribal war bands and, in an era of constant warfare, the transition from tribe to supertribe, grouped under cunning warlords, was well under way.

These vigorous northern 'barbarians' were the destroyers of the Western Empire of Rome. It was they who delivered the *coup de grâce* to the dying colossus in the south, subsequently creating medieval Europe, the feudal system and chivalry. It was their direct descendants who were the knights and men-at-arms. In every sense, they were the creators of the modern world; it is ironic that most of us know virtually nothing about them.

The Warrior

An essential factor in early Germanic and Celtic warfare was the warrior's own large, powerful frame. The German proper was a variant of the earlier Nordic type introduced by the Indo-European invasion; he was, in general, larger, due to racial mixture with the great northern hunters still surviving in northern Europe from the last Ice Age. The body was heavier and thicker than the pure Nordic type, with a large braincase. He was characteristically blond or rufous, as seen in his modern descendants and noted by numerous early writers. The two exceptions to this general picture were the Alemanni and the Franks, who resembled the people they eventually settled among, the Celts.

Diet was heavy and rich in protein, broadly including pork, beef and fish (fresh and salted), mutton, venison, game, bread, beer and dairy produce.

Everyday dress varied from group to group. The overall costume, however, was the same throughout the north—a simple tunic, long trousers and cloak, which was usually of a blackish or dark brown wool. The tunic reached the knees and had either long or short sleeves. Several tunics could be worn at once, supplemented with fur and pelts of different kinds in cold weather. In summer, of course, upper garments were often left off altogether. Linen was known but was an

Longbows found at Nydam and dated to the late 4th century A.D.; about 2m long and made of yew, they bear a close affinity to the great English warbow of the Middle Ages. The arrows, of pinewood and hazel, measure between 68cm and 85 cm; they were found in bundles. (Not to scale)

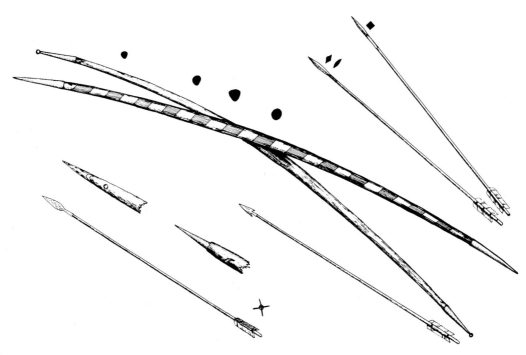

expensive import from the south, and was, for that reason, only worn by the wealthier or far-travelled tribesmen. Trousers were held up by rawhide thonging; sometimes cross-thonging held them into the lower legs or ankles. Trousers were made in wool, as well as fur and skins. Knee-length breeches, when worn, were combined with a tight leg covering. Belts of varied thickness were worn at the waist or across the shoulder, sometimes both. Straps could be used for carrying the shield.

The cloak was about five feet across, rectangular or circular, of woven wool, sometimes having a fur lining. Cloaks entirely of skins were also worn. They were secured with *fibulae* or brooches of differing kinds, some types being more popular among some tribes than others. Clothing of the lower class was of the roughest kind—the simplest woven tunics or dressed skins. Shoes were of a very simple design, in some ways similar to the moccasins of the North American Indian, turned up over the foot from the sole and tied at the ankle.

Hair was often left long, being sometimes plaited, gathered into a top-knot or twisted into the curious knot peculiar to the Suebian tribes such as the Marcomanni and Quadi. Beards were usually but not always worn. Tribesmen normally went bareheaded, but a woollen or fur cap might be worn in cold weather. Razors, combs, scissors and tweezers of early date have been found in Germanic territory. The rough woollen cloth used by the Germans was woven in plain colours, of striped or other geometric design. Dyeing was carried out with vegetable substances, a skill which had existed in the north since the Bronze Age, if not before. Red was obtained from madder root, yellow from saffron flowers and the stalks or leaves of weld, blue from woad, green from what is now known as 'dyers' greenweed'. Many garments were also left in their natural hue—wool has a number of natural shades, ranging from almost pure white, through fawn, brown and grey to black.

Bracelets, earrings, armlets, necklets, beads and rings were worn by both sexes, to a greater or lesser degree, according to taste.

Strong influences from the rich Bronze Age of northern Europe, and also the influence of the Celts and Scythians, were present in Germanic

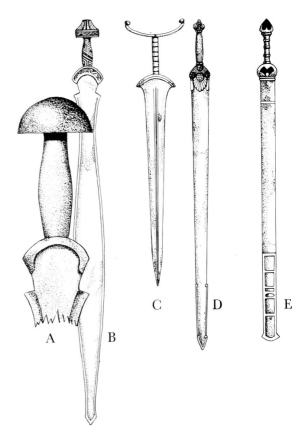

Celtic swords and hilts: (A) 'Mushroom' style pommel, from a large Halstatt sword (B) 'Mexican hat' style pommel from an early Halstatt sword, 108cm long, dated to the 8th century B.C. (C) Late Halstatt iron sword with 'antler' or 'antennae' hilt, 72cm long, 7th century B.C. (D) and (E), La Tène iron swords and scabbards, both 5th to 6th centuries B.C., one 90cm and the other 88cm long.

culture. Roman culture played an ever-increasing part in northern European society after the Celtic collapse in Gaul. In their rôle as a source of weapons and luxury goods, the Romans began their long involvement with the Germans as they faced them across the northern frontiers.

Of the Warrior

'. . . Who these people were and from what part of the world they had set out, to fall on Gaul and Italy like a thundercloud, no one knew; for they had no contact with the southern races, and had already travelled a very great way. The likeliest guess seemed to be that they were some of the German tribes, whose territory extends up to the northern ocean. This conjecture was based on their great size, the light blue colour of their eyes, and the fact that the German word for plunderers

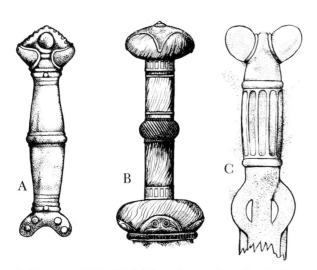

La Tène sword hilts: (A) Solid cast bronze, from Cumberland, England (B) Tinned bronze fittings on wood, from Dorset, England (C) From a bas-relief at Pergamon, Turkey.

is "Cimbri". . . . As for the barbarians, they were so full of confidence in themselves and of contempt for their enemies that they went out of their way to give, quite unnecessarily, exhibitions of their strength and daring. They went naked through snow-storms, climbed to the summits of the mountains, through the ice and snow drifts, and, from there, came tobogganing down on their broad shields, sliding over the slippery slopes and the deep crevasses.' (From the passage on the Cimbri and Teutons, *Fall of the Roman Republic* by Plutarch.)

'. . . The Germans wear no breast plates or helmets. Even their shields are not reinforced with iron or leather, but are merely plaited wickerwork or painted boards. Spears, of a sort, are limited to their front rank. The rest have clubs, burnt at the ends or with short metal points. Physically, they are formidable and good for a short rush. But they cannot stand being hurt . . .' (Part of an eve of battle speech to his troops by Germanicus, 16 A.D.)

'. . . In their war with the Emperor Commodus, the Buri, a small tribe of Germans of the middle Danube, had to ask the Emperor on many occasions for a truce in order to replenish their scanty supply of weapons. They are a tall race, clad in close-fitting garments with a belt round the waist; they hurl their axes and cast their spears with great force, never missing their aim. They manage their shields with great skill, rushing on

their enemy so fast that they seem to fly faster than their javelins.' (Agathius, 405 A.D., writing of the Franks.)

'. . . A Gothic horseman's lance went right through a Roman cavalryman. The Goth slowly raised the dripping lance, with the armoured Roman kicking and vomiting on the end of it.' (Procopius, secretary to the great general of the Eastern Empire, Belisarius, 6th century A.D.)

'. . . Vandal cavalry fight with spear and sword. They have little or no defensive armour, [and] are not good infantrymen, archers or javelineers. Their army was very similar to that of the Ostrogoths, though the Goths had a large infantry force.' (Sidonius Apollinaris. 430–480 A.D.)

'. . . Drinking bouts, lasting a day and night, are not considered in any way disgraceful . . . No one in Germany finds vice amusing, or calls it 'up-to-date' to debauch and be debauched . . . If they approve, they clash spears. No form of approval can carry more honour than praise expressed by arms. . . .'

'. . . On the field of battle it is a disgrace to the chief to be surpassed in valour by his companions or to the companions not to come up in valour to their chief. As for leaving the battle alive after the chief has fallen, *that* means lifelong infamy and shame. To defend and protect him, to put down one's own acts of heroism to his credit, that is what they really mean by allegiance. The chiefs fight for victory, the companions for their chief. Many noble youths, if their land is stagnating in a protracted peace, deliberately seek out other tribes where some war is afoot. The Germans have no taste for peace; renown is easier won among perils, and you cannot maintain a large body of companions except by violence and war. . . .'

'. . . You will find it harder to persuade a German to plough the land and await its annual produce with patience than to challenge a foe and earn the prize of wounds. He thinks it spiritless and slack to gain by sweat what he can buy with blood.' (Tacitus. *Germania.*)

These tantalizing glimpses of north European barbarians, seen through the eyes of civilized southerners, are helpful in giving life to the more immediate relics unearthed by the archaeologist. It should be remembered that not all had witnessed German warriors at first hand; most Romans would have seen their first Germans only if auxiliary troops were posted near their town or had appeared in the arena.

Weapons

Economically the Germanic tribes were peasants, living mainly from stock-rearing (cattle, sheep and goats) and farming. As time went by, isolated farms became groups of farms, developing into hamlets and, eventually, villages. The skills of early German craftsmen showed unaccountable limitations in some directions. This was always evident in the weaponry of the early tribesmen. Roman assessment of the Germanic peoples was, above all, as warriors. With a few notable exceptions, Roman writers had no personal contact with them, and some of their observations may be suspect. Archaeology, however, has supplied a large and detailed amount of German weapon history. Because of the relative paucity of native innovation the Germans, particularly those in the west, were influenced to a large degree by the Celtic Halstatt and La Tène periods of culture. After the Roman conquest of Gaul, Roman weapons played an increasing part in the arming of Germanic war bands, until, in the late Empire, a steady flow of arms northward was sustained by illicit arms deals, loot from Roman arsenals and armies, and equipment brought home by the large numbers of Germans who had served in the Roman army. A broad approximation of phases in weaponry among the ancient Germans, based on recent archaeological evidence, is as follows:

Celtic: Halstatt culture: 7th cent. B.C. Swords of bronze and iron, native iron lances and axes; a period during which very large Celtic weapons were in use—heavy swords, spearheads reaching 75cm in length.

Celtic: Late Halstatt: early 5th cent. B.C. The importance of the sword is overtaken by that of the short, single-edged knife. Ordinary warriors are equipped with a lance and shield of sorts. Javelins furnished with a throwing thong are in use; the axe is more common in eastern German territories.

Celtic: first la Tène culture: late 5th cent. B.C. The

Wooden shields from Hjortspring; the 'barleycorn' bosses are also of wood. These shields, dated to the 1st century B.C., measure 88cm × 50cm, and 66cm × 30cm. Also, two German iron *sax* knives, both about 46cm long.

The northern limits of the La Tène Culture.

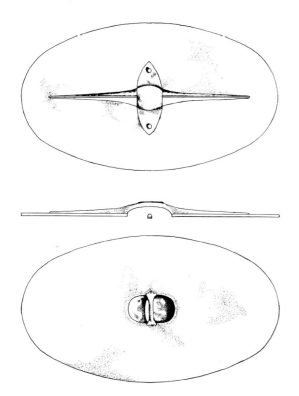

Diagram of an oval Celtic shield made of oak planks, covered with leather and backed with felt; it would probably be finished with a painted design. About 1.1m long, it is 1.2cm thick at the centre and less towards the rim. The spine of shaped wood is hollowed out to receive the warrior's fist as he grasps the handle—normally reinforced with an iron bracing strip—at the rear. The boss itself has an iron reinforcing strip.

(Top to bottom) An Anglo-Saxon *sax*, 6th century A.D.; a Frankish *sax* of the same period; and a rusted iron *sax* about 50cm long, found at Chadlington, Oxfordshire.

beginning of the Celtic La Tène culture sees the Germans in possession of very few swords. The impression gained is that, in parts of Germany, the long sword is virtually unknown. Ordinary warriors are equipped with local variants of spear type, shield and dagger. Spearheads measure 12cm to 26cm.

Celtic: second La Tène phase: 3rd to 2nd cent. B.C. No change.in armament evident. At Hjortspring a large wooden boat was discovered preserved in the peat. Classified as a votive deposit and dated to around the late 3rd century B.C., it was accompanied by 138 iron and 31 bone spears, 150 shields and six swords. The shields were all of Celtic patterns—a long, oval type, measuring 88cm × 50cm, and the more common rectangular type, measuring 66cm × 30cm. Towards the end of this period several changes seem to have affected German war bands. The *sax*, a one-edged weapon of varying length, was introduced; its origin is unknown. A few warriors were equipped with La Tène swords—they may have been specialist swordsmen. These men were less common in eastern Germanic territories. The use of Celtic spears, javelins and shields is still evident, the latter with iron bosses. All weapons are light and sparing in the use of iron, confirming an iron-poor society.

Roman period: 1st cent. A.D. Swordsmen number about one in ten among Germanic warriors of this period. There is no evidence of armour or

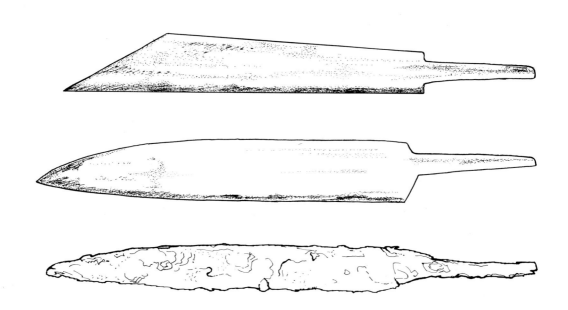

helmets, except in the case of a very few chieftains. Shields are round, rectangular or sexagonal, dished, and with a prominent projecting boss and iron or bronze edging. Small round or oval shields were used by the cavalry.

Roman period: 2nd cent. A.D. Roman and German equipment begins to appear together in a number of areas. Mail garments and Roman swords of the *gladius* type, with ring pommel, and an increase in the use of axes, especially the throwing-axe.

Roman period: 3rd cent. A.D. Roman weapons continue to find their way into northern lands, especially in the more northerly territories. Swordsmen probably number about one in every four warriors. Swords of Roman *spatha* type, together with other Roman types, increasingly find their way into German hands. In the peat bogs at Ejsbol North, 160 shields, 191 spears, 203 barbed javelins, 60 swords, 60 belts and 62 knives were found. Roman cavalry helmets of parade type were used in a few cases probably as marks of rank.

Roman period: 4th cent. A.D. Shields seem to be rarely carried at this period. When found, the bosses are of the Roman domed variety. The old German spiked types are evidently out of fashion.

Owing to widespread cremation of the dead among the northern barbarians the discovered cemeteries, many of them very large, afford little information except for those interested in pottery. Frankish warrior graves in what was northern Gaul and the Rhineland, dated from the mid-4th to the 5th century A.D., are furnished with spears, throwing-axes and an occasional sword. These warriors were probably federate soldiers employed by the Romans. One richly furnished grave of a Germanic officer found in a late Roman cemetery contained a sword, a belt, an oval silver plate and a shield originally covered with purple leather and gold foil plates; the boss had been sheathed in silver-gilt. Other weapons included were a throwing axe, ten spears and a larger spear inlaid with silver. Other Frankish graves in Belgium contain belt fittings and buckles, spears and throwing-axes.

Bows

Well-made longbows were found at Nydam, in the territory of the Angles. They are about two metres long, made of yew, with stave ends tipped with iron or antler ferrules, and the hand-holds bound with fine thread. Arrows were about 68cm to 85cm long.

Germanic bows, dating from about 100 A.D. to 350 A.D., were made of yew and fir wood. They were recognisable long bows of deep 'D' section. It is probable that, like the English longbow of later ages, these were 'compound' bows a combination of the sapwood, which resists stretching, for the back, and heat-wood, resistant to compression, for the belly or inside of the bow. Staves found at Vimose, Kragehul and Nydam measure from 168cm to 198cm. Although used only to a limited degree by Germanic groups in the British Isles, and even less by those settled in Gaul, the bow was used to advantage by other Germans.

As stated above, self bows and a few composite bows were used by the Alemanni. True longbows were present in northern bog deposits. Dated from the 2nd to the 4th centuries A.D., these weapons were probably developed by the Germans themselves. Some arrow piles found seem to be designed to puncture armour.

(Left and right) A Roman cavalry sword of unusual shape, and its scabbard, from Gotland; between them, the hilt of a Roman *gladius* from Thorsbjerg.

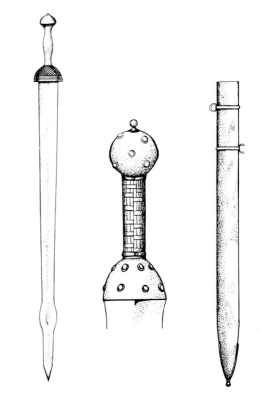

Roman cavalry sword, length 102cm overall; and below it, a Roman *gladius* with the late 'ring' pommel, length 60cm overall. Both are dated to about the 2nd century A.D. and were found at Vimose in Denmark.

A large part of the Visigothic army, as mentioned elsewhere, were archers and spearmen. Their cavalry were composed of chieftains and their companions.

Bowmen also formed an important element in Ostrogothic armies; as with other German bowmen, a very small number of composite bows may have been used, but the overwhelming majority would be self or compound bows. (Their cavalry were armed with spears and swords derived from those of the Sarmatians; Ostrogothic nobles owned lavish, gold-decorated, heavy slashing swords, mounted with almondins.) The longbows found at Vimose, Kragehul and Nydam, dated to 100–350 A.D., have previously been noted. The bow used extensively by all steppe nomads, including the Sarmatians and Huns, was the powerful, reflexed, composite bow. Its stave is constructed of laminated materials of different origin, such as wood, sinew and horn. When unstrung the bow forms the silhouette of the letter 'C', sometimes with the ends forming a cross. When strung, the 'C' was opened back against its natural curve and held that way by the string—thus, the bow 'coiled' for action.

Early Swords

Early Celtic iron swords follow the general pattern of previous bronze examples, which were still in use well after the introduction of iron. The first iron swords manufactured in Europe were long, slashing weapons; in the opinion of most experts, they were primarily designed for use by chariot-borne warriors. Some of the weapons belonging to the Halstatt culture were so large that there is some doubt that they were made for actual use. The hilts are generally very distinctive, having a pommel similar to a Mexican hat. Examples include hilts of horn or ivory, decorated with gold or amber, a few have a mushroom-like profile.

Late Halstatt swords, introduced about B.C. 600, were fashioned after examples of Greek or Etruscan provenance; some indeed may be imports from the south. They were smaller than the great middle Halstatt swords, and were designed to be used for both slashing and stabbing, in that they carried a point. Their hilts fall into two main patterns, 'antennae' and 'anthropomorphic'. The former followed an old late Bronze Age pattern; the latter took the stylised form of a spreadeagled man. The blades of these weapons were made of iron, forged to harden by introducing carbon in various ways, finishing with a carburised

(Top) A long, heavy Gothic cavalry sword from Tamin in southern Russia, 5th century A.D.—partly restored in this sketch. (Bottom) A sword recovered from Kragehul Bog, Denmark; it has bronze scabbard mounts and hilt, and is dated to the 5th century A.D. (Not to scale.)

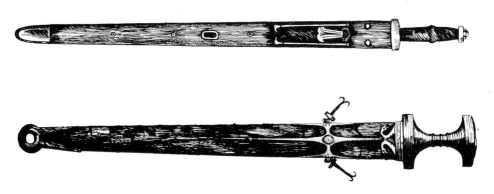

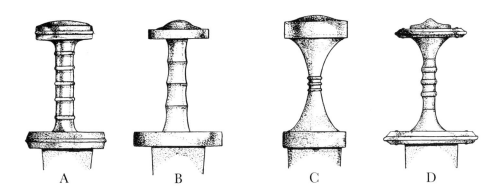

A   B   C   D

iron of indifferent quality. Although there are notable exceptions, most Celtic swords were made in this way.

Early La Tène swords were introduced about B.C. 450. They have pointed blades about 55cm to 65cm long; there is one known example 80cm long. *La Tène (II) period swords* date from c. B.C. 250 to 120. They measure about 75–80cm and have rounder points. *The final La Tène phase swords*, dated from B.C. 120 to the defeat of the Gallic tribes by Rome, were longer than those of the two previous periods. They are between 60cm and 90cm long; a few were pointed but most were blunt-ended.

Pattern Welded Blades

In the early 1st century A.D. a new process, which we call pattern-welding, was invented by European swordsmiths. The process was complicated, but not so long drawn out as many earlier tempering methods. The central section of the blade was prepared by forging narrow billets of high-quality carburised iron, twisting them together in pairs, laying the twists side by side, welding them, and finally adding further strips of carburised iron to the sides and welding them to form the cutting edges. At this stage the blade was a long, flat, oblong billet, which had to be filed and ground down to the desired form. It was then burnished and etched with an acid such as tannin, urine, sour beer or vinegar; when the central section and fuller were polished, a pattern having the appearance of a snake's back emerged, a result of the twisting carried out at an earlier stage in the sword's manufacture. According to the method used in this grouping and twisting phase, many variations of pattern were possible.

Sword hilts of the Mignation period: (A) From about 150 A.D. (B) From about 400 A.D. (C) From about 350 A.D. — a Northern pattern (D) From about 500 A.D.

Sword rings and 'life-stones'

On the pommels of some of these swords, rings, mostly decorated, are attached. These are believed to be special gifts from a grateful chieftain. Some scabbards have large beads attached to them, either of pottery, glass, meerschaum, crystal or, rarely, gold set with stones, and occasionally with gold or silver mounts. These are amulets—charms to bring good luck—and were believed to have the magical property to heal wounds made by the sword to which they were attached.

Swords of the Heroic Period

'When the enemy had taken possession of two camps and an immense booty, they destroyed, under new and strange oaths, all that had fallen into their hands. The clothes were torn and thrown away, gold and silver thrown into the river, the ring armour of the men cut to pieces, the accoutrements of the horses destroyed, the horses themselves thrown into the water, and the men, with ropes around their necks, suspended from the trees, so that there was no more booty for the victors than there was mercy for the conquered.'

This extract from a history written about B.C. 100, by the Roman historian Orosius, deals with the Celtic invasion by the Cimbri and Teutones. It highlights the religious obligation felt by the Celts and Germans to sacrifice 'killed' enemy possessions, leaving us with priceless deposits in the bogs of northern Europe to supplement those found in the graves of Germanic warriors. Swords of this period are found in both types of deposit,

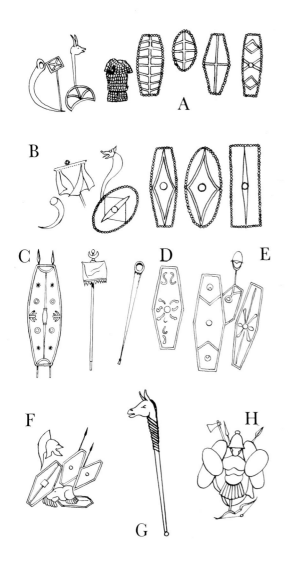

A

B

C
D
E

F

G

H

A selection of barbarian arms and armour and other trophies, taken from Roman coin reverses. These coin designs, illustrating in simple style samples of the booty taken in triumphant military expeditions, allow tentative associations to be made by comparing the known date of the coin with the known contemporary campaigns: probable associations are shown here bracketed.

(A) From a *sestertius* of Marcus Aurelius, dated to 180 A.D.: horn, plaque, monster-headed trumpet, *pelta*-type shield, corselet, and shields of curve-sided oblong, small oval, hexagonal and narrow, curve-sided shapes. (Sarmatians, Quadi and Marcomanni)

(B) From an *aurius* of Marcus Aurelius, dated to 180 A.D.: horn, vexillum, large monster-headed trumpet/standard, and shields of small oval, curve-sided oblong, oval and oblong shapes. (Quadi and Marcomanni)

(C) From a coin of Domitian, dated to 90 A.D.: a long Celtic-type shield with two spears, a vexillum and a long trumpet. (Quadi)

(D) From a coin of Domitian, dated to 90 A.D.: a hexagonal shield. (Quadi or Marcomanni)

(E) From a coin of Domitian, date unknown: three hexagonal shields and a helmet. (Quadi, Marcomanni)

(F) From a coin of Titus, dated to 81 A.D.: German shields, three hexagonal and one octagonal; a helmet of the old Romano-Etruscan type, a muscle cuirass and two spears. (Hermanduri and Marcomanni)

(G) From a *sestertius* of T. Decius, dated to 250 A.D.; a horse-head standard. (Gothic)

(H) From a *solidus* of Crispus, dated to 319 A.D.: a trophy of arms comprising a muscle cuirass and conical helmet, probably both Roman, two round-ended oblong shields, two smaller oval shields, a battleaxe, two spears, a cloak and a composite bow with a ringed string. (Alemanni)

but are present in comparatively few graves.

Roman swords are represented in the bog finds by the short *gladius* and long cavalry *spatha*. One interesting hilt, belonging to a Roman *gladius*, was found at Thorsbjerg, South Jutland. It is similar to one in the British Museum and another found at Pompeii. Its bronze hilt has little bosses on guard and pommel, with a grip covered in fine woven bronze thread braiding. Another example, complete with its scabbard, was found in Gotland. It has a swelling on either side of the blade, just above the point. *Gladii* dated to the 2nd century A.D. have pommels in the shape of a large ring. Several Roman cavalry swords have turned up in the bog deposits.

Besides the Roman swords, Thorsbjerg produced swords of native manufacture. All are double-edged, with bronze- and silver-covered wooden handles. The wooden scabbards bore metal mounts. Also found were a thick sword belt; bronze and iron belt buckles; bows, arrows and shields. These latter were circular and flat, measuring 54cm to 108cm in diameter, with most grips and fastenings of bronze but some of iron. Axes found in this deposit were mounted on wooden shafts 59cm to 85cm long; spears were mounted on shafts 81cm, 250cm, 273cm and 295cm long. Harness for both driving and riding was found, together with much jewellery, tools, amber dice, bowls, spoons, jugs and knives. Garments included mail shirts, gold-plated bronze circular pectoral plates, and a converted Roman cavalry parade helmet covered in silver. Roman coins found included some of Septimus Severus, dated 194 A.D.

At Vimose in Denmark 67 swords were found; most were double-edged, but some were single-edged *saxes*. Of 1,000 spears, five were mounted on shafts 198cm, 264cm, 280cm, and 302cm long; some of these spears had inlays of gold, silver and bronze. Mail was recovered, some of it gilded, together with a complete mail shirt 92cm long; there were also examples of scabbard furniture,

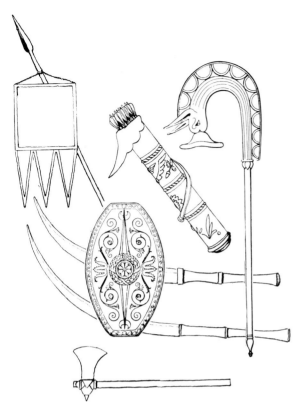

150 knives, buckles, fibulae, buttons, harness, scythe blades, keys, scissors, needles, nails, a millstone, an anvil, hammers, chisels, files, pincers, combs, brooches, beads and four amber dice. This find is dated to the late 4th century A.D.

At Kragehul, also in Denmark, were found ten pattern-welded swords, with spears set in a circular fence. The find is dated to the 4th and 5th centuries A.D.

The four-ship burial at Nydam is of great importance. It contained two small ships which were beyond reconstruction, and two larger ones in a much better state of preservation. Among the associated finds were 106 double-edged swords, 93 of them pattern-welded; silvered sheaths and bone and cast bronze hilts; 552 spears, some inlaid with gold, and arrows. All dated from 200 A.D. to 350 A.D.

Most Germanic swords fall into one or other of the classifications worked out by the Swedish expert Elis Behmer; the hilts of four types occurring frequently in our period are illustrated.

ABOVE **Dacian arms and standards, from various Roman bas-reliefs: not to scale. A dagged banner on a spear; two battle-scythes—*falxes*; a quiver, shield and battleaxe; and a carnyx-style standard with a ferrule.**

Helmets from Dacia and Asia.(A)–(E): 'Phrygian' type, from the pedestal of Trajan's Column. (F) and (G): Phrygian helmets. (H) Sarmatian helmet, from Trajan's Column. (I) and (J): Domed helmets, from the pedestal of Trajan's Column. (Not to scale.)

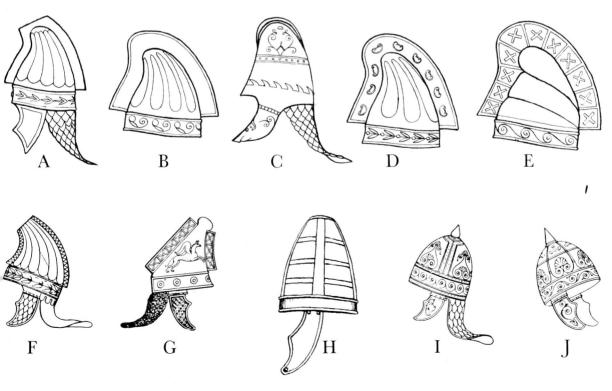

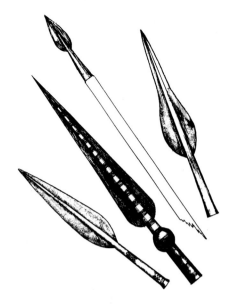

German iron spearheads, 4th to 6th centuries A.D.

Dacian Arms and Armour

The column erected in the Forum of Rome and dedicated to the Emperor Trajan in 113 A.D. illustrates in a spiral ribbon of reliefs the phases and main incidents of his conquest of Dacia. The square pedestal at the base of the column carried examples of arms and armour in confused abundance. The monument, in two halves, can best be seen in England at the Victoria and Albert Museum, where excellent full-scale plaster casts exist. They were taken during the 19th century, and give a

Helmets from the tomb-carvings of A. Julius Pompilius, 175 A.D., at the time of the Marcomannic Wars. (A) Roman battle helmet (B) Damaged carving of Roman cavalry sports helmet (C) Curious helmet of indistinct type. These are thought to depict helmets worn by the enemy in this campaign.

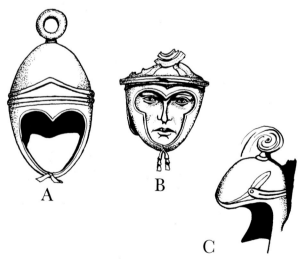

A   B

C

better presentation of the reliefs than the more corroded original in Rome. On confronting the highly-decorated, carved sides of the pedestal, it becomes obvious that the formal abbreviations of costume and weapons used on the column are absent: on the column we have narrative, on the pedestal we are looking at graphic examples of the masses of equipment captured by Roman forces from their opponents in Dacia, sculpted from actual examples of the trophies. In their original condition the bas-reliefs were painted in realistic colours, with details of armour and weapons added in metal. Periodic renewal of the paint was carried out during the life of the Empire.

The cluttered abundance of these impressive trophies begs the question 'Which piece of equipment belongs to which group of barbarians involved in the campaigns?' Perhaps a more relevant question is 'Are the carvings in fact representative of the arms of only one people, the gifted and proud Geto-Dacians, who Trajan had destroyed during a deliberate campaign of Roman expansion into central Europe?' Ancient Dacia, in the 2nd century, embraced Transylvania, Banat and Valachia proper. The true Dacians were a people of Thracian descent. German, Celtic and Iranian elements occupied territories in the north-western and north-eastern parts of Dacia. Cultural elements of Hellenic, Scythian, Celtic and Roman origin were absorbed in a rich amalgam.

Shields

The dominant articles on the pedestal reliefs are the large, richly decorated, oval shields. They are the only type of body shield shown; all are of uniform shape and style of decoration. The exceptions are examples which are covered in a scale pattern. Another example of an unusual Dacian design is found on an oval shield carried by a man in Dacian costume on another Trajanic relief which was moved to the Arch of Constantine. It has four monster-headed trumpets radiating from the central boss, and two Celtic-type torques of twisted metal which, together with the monster trumpets shown in groups all over the pedestal, may illustrate Celtic influence.

With these exceptions, Dacian shields, as shown on the carvings, are heavily decorated with floriate, braided, geometric and planetary designs, as well as the ancient Thracian shield

known as the *Pelta* (this symbol is used in normal and distorted form). These shields are very large and, it would appear from the carvings, flat, the patterns being in proud relief to facilitate periodic painting. The bosses are hemispherical with round boss plates, both being decorated. I suggest that the Thracian lunate shield motif, repeatedly used on these shields, confirms them as Dacian or Geto-Dacian.

Helmets

The helmets on the reliefs fall into two categories: one with a neat, rounded, cone-shaped shell, the other with its apex curved forward into the characteristic 'Phrygian' peak. Both are highly decorated in the same fashion as the shields on the column base. It is the decoration on one of the solid crests running over one of these helmets, together with the close general resemblance to various examples of helmets worn by ancient Phrygians shown in art, and the obvious connection between them, which leads me to suggest that the 'Phygian'-type helmets may well be a variety peculiar to the Dacians.

The Dacians, as stated above, were a Thracian

(Left) A tombstone at Dollendorf near Bonn, shows this Germanic warrior—probably a Frank. He is combing his hair, and his sword is clearly shown; both were considered virility symbols, and were proudly displayed. (Right) Finely sculpted profile of a German chieftain from the tomb of A. Julius Pompilius, now in the National Museum, Terme.

BELOW **Late Roman military belt fittings. (Top) This example** of ancillary strap attachments and stiffeners is from a grave at Dorchester, England. Probably general issue by the late Empire period, they are usually associated with German auxiliary troops of the Roman army. (Bottom) A reconstructed belt, with strap attachments, stiffeners and plates, from a German warrior's grave at Rhenan, Holland.

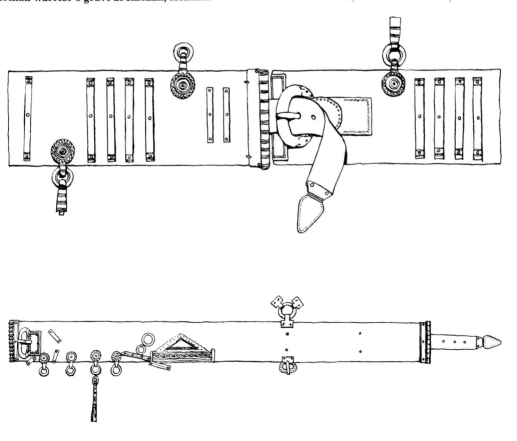

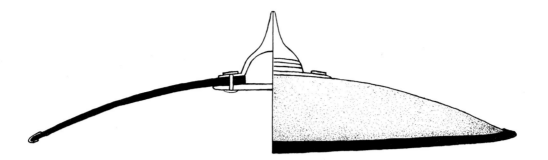

Diagram of an Anglo-Saxon shield, typical of the round shields carried by other Germanic tribesmen. Made of limewood, it is about 5cm thick and 90cm across. Thin, shaped boards were covered with linen or leather; the central recess, with an off-centre metal handle, was covered with a large iron boss; and the rim was of iron or bronze, perhaps sometimes of leather. As well as the concave type, flat, round shields were also used. The face was often reinforced with metal strips, and normally painted with simple or elaborate decorations.

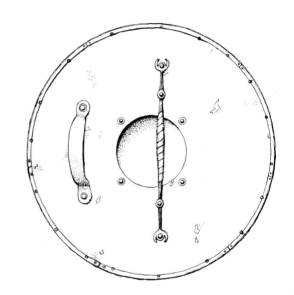

Reconstruction of the inside of an Anglo-Saxon shield, showing forearm strap and hand-grip.

people, as were the Phrygians and those Thracians living north of the Greek states throughout the classical period. The distinct lunate shield used by Thracian infantrymen, the *pelta*, illustrated frequently in Greek art, is present on the solid crest of a 'Phrygian'-type helmet as a running pattern, as shown on the pedestal reliefs; this motif was used repeatedly on the large oval shields. It would be very neat to see in the plainer, domed helmets Scytho-Sarmatian examples, but they resemble the construction of these in only one way—they are conical. The helmets worn by Iranian armoured horsemen on the column and other Roman reliefs are of a composite construction. The banded floriate designs decorating the non-'Phrygian' helmets on the pedestal duplicate the designs shown on the 'Phrygian' helmets. That these helmets represent a newer type of Dacian helmet is a more probable proposition.

Body Armour

This is represented in three varieties—mail, leaf-scale and banded construction. These examples give no indication of their origin or ownership at the time of capture, with the possible exception of the corselet of banded armour, which may not be European.

Dacian Costume

This is more easily identified in the tunic and cloak outfits seen worn on the column and depicted among the trophies on the pedestal. Dacians are not seen on the column wearing body armour or

helmets. Lack of any defence other than the shield must have been characteristic of most of the Geto-Dacians but not of the whole nation, although all are shown unarmoured in a conventional style. Swords are well represented on the reliefs. One weapon, of late Celtic La Tène type, hangs from a belt on a coat of leaf armour. Other long swords with plainer, *spatha*-type guards and hilts have plated belts attached to the scabbard.

The *draco*, a metallic standard in the form of a dragon head with its mouth open, attached to a tubular, fabric body of brilliant hue, was used by many ancient peoples including Dacians, Iranians and Germans. Those shown on the pedestal could belong to any of these groups. *Vexilla*, ancient banners, shown on the column friezes and pedestal, may be examples of recaptured Roman *signa*, or may belong to any of the participating barbarians. One example, attached to a spear,

looks very un-Roman; it carries three large 'dags' at its lower edge.

Weapons

Spears and javelins are of standard types and give no hint as to their provenance. Battleaxes of a distinct type are present, as are the terrible *falxes*. It is postulated that these scythe-like weapons were so effective in early actions between Roman and Dacian infantry that special Roman armour, based on antique patterns, was devised, and shields were reinforced. Both composite and self bows are present on the reliefs, the self bow being more numerous on the carvings but little-shown on the column, where Dacians and Sarmatians are both shown using reflex bows. Quivers are of a lidded, tubular shape, highly decorated. Trumpets, after the fashion of the Celtic *carnyx*, in the shape of monster serpents, are shown in groups. Some examples, however, seem to be designed as standards for carrying, having a large finial at the butt end.

If this analysis is generally correct, then it would seem that the base of Trajan's Column carries bas-reliefs of armour, arms and other equipment wholly or overwhelmingly belonging to the Dacian people, the target of Trajan's campaigns. Some authorities may see in the presence of various pieces associated with cultures further to the east, especially the coat of banded armour, trophies of erstwhile ownership by Iranian Roxolani. I would agree that this is a reasonable theory; but would it not be possible for leading warriors among the Geto-Dacians to own pieces of armour not made in Europe?

Warfare

Prior to the conquest and pacification of Gaul by Roman forces, German tribes proper began moving south-west. By the early 1st century A.D. they were in the Rhineland area. The people settled at this time between the Aller in the east and the Oise in the west are believed to have been an aboriginal group of 'old' Europeans, neither

The general distribution of major Germanic groups in about 100 A.D.

Wars, Tacitus wrote his *Germania*[1], a study of the Germans written in about 98 A.D. In the passage describing the arming of warriors, he says: 'Only a few have swords or spears. The lances that they carry—*frameae* is the native word—have short and sharp heads, but are so narrow and easy to handle that the same weapon serves for fighting hand to hand or at a distance. The horseman demands no more than his shield and spear, but the infantry-man has also javelins for throwing, several to each man, and he can hurl them to a great distance.'

This description accords well with archaeological evidence dated to this time. Whether *frameae* had short, narrow heads by choice or simply because of the tribes' shortage of iron is not made clear by the historian. Bodies found preserved in the peat bogs of northern Europe, dated to this period, are dressed exactly the same as the Germans shown on Roman monumental remains. With the exception of a very few individuals, German body defences—apart from the shield—were non-existent at the time of their early encounters with Imperial troops. The usual tactic adopted at this time was to attack at a headlong rush, in wedge formation, so as to close in quickly, thus nullifying the murderous volleys of legionary *pila*: the 'Furore Teutonicus' of legend.

In the early years of the 1st century A.D. Rome decided to rationalise the northern frontier by annexing Germany up to the Elbe. The closing move, against the Marcomanni, was frustrated when the new provinces in north Germany flared into revolt. The three legions stationed in the area, the XVII, XVIII and XIX, were annihilated in a series of ambushes in the Teutoburger Wald in 9 A.D. The German leader, Hermann (Arminius), chief of the Cherusci, had served in the Roman army and had used his knowledge of its operational limitations in boggy, heavily wooded areas. Hermann aspired to more permanent power than that afforded to a war leader, and was subsequently destroyed by political enemies at home. The indisputable outcome of this disaster was that Roman plans for the eventual control of all of Germania were permanently abandoned.

Celtic nor Germanic, speaking a pre-Indo-European tongue. Their replacement by a more pugnacious people was almost certainly recognized by Roman frontier intelligence, which may have triggered the Augustan campaigns. Tribes such as the Chatti, Cherusci, Chamavi, Chattvarii, Chamari, Angrivarii, Ampsivarii, etc., were followed by the Alemanni, Goths, Gepids, Franks, Vandals, Bajuvara, Thuringians and Saxons.

Probably drawing heavily on the experiences of men returned from the German campaigns of Augustus, and on Pliny the Elder's *The German*

Two iron axeheads, the elevations on the left from a find at Brandenburg, and those on the right from a find at Weissenfels.

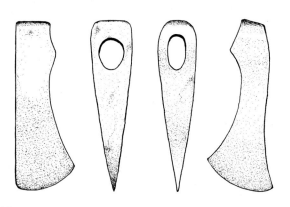

---

[1] Pliny's book is now lost; this is the more tragic since we know that the author had himself served on the frontier.

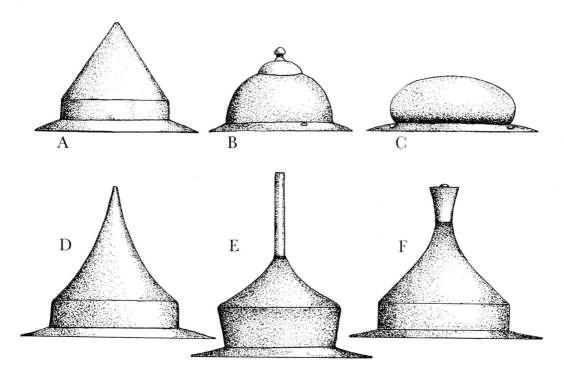

German iron shield bosses from (A) Hamburg (B) Gotland (C) Gotland (D) Hamfelde (E) Vimose (F) Gotland

Germanicus, the nephew of the Emperor Tiberius, conducted a series of short campaigns in Lower Germany, making some amends for the destruction of the three-legion garrison of the area by paying honour to them in their place of death. The Empire was kept within its frontiers and stood on the defensive in the north. Caligula's idiot dreams of conquest in Germany came and went until other antics took his interest.

During the civil wars of 68 to 69 A.D., Gallic tribes of the north-east, with German allies, destroyed Roman forces on the Rhine and announced an 'Empire of the Gauls'. Roman forces moved swiftly to eradicate this Gallic empire. Vespasian and his sons then closed the

'Spangenhelm' composite helmets of the Migration period. (Left) Iron helmet of a Roman auxiliary soldier of the 3rd century A.D., found in Holland. (Centre) Gothic helmet from the battlefield of Tolbiacum, 5th century A.D.; the shell is of iron, with decorative gilded copper skinning. (Right) Helmet from a 6th century warrior's grave in Alsace—probably an heirloom of earlier date.

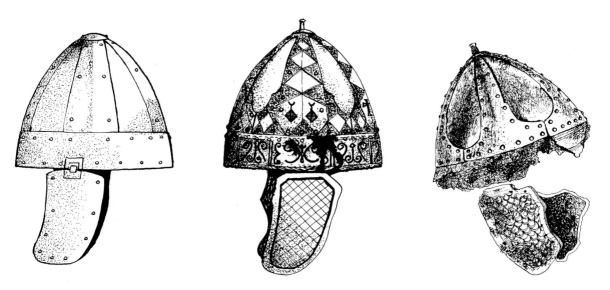

dangerous gap between the Rhine and Danube with a deep defence system. After Domitian had halted the migrating Chatti on the middle Rhine, during a series of bitterly fought campaigns in 83 and 88 A.D., Upper and Lower Germany settled down to a period of quiet, ably administered by Trajan. Legions could now be transferred from the Rhine to the Danube. Eastern German tribes began to attract Roman military interest when the great Marcomannic chieftain, Maraboduus, created a large confederacy of tribes, after his own people, together with the Quadi, had driven the Boii from Bohemia. He eventually escaped to sanctuary in Ravenna in 17 A.D., when fellow Germans reacted against his growing power.

Thracians

During the great migrations of an earlier period, Indo-European groups of warriors and their families moved into large areas of Europe. One of these closely related groups occupied territory in south-eastern Europe and, eventually, parts of the Near East and east-central Europe. These were the Thracians. In the 1st century the Thracians of southern Europe were separated from their more northerly kin, the Dacians. The Thracians within the Roman frontier became famous for their recruitment into the Roman cavalry.

German standards: (Left) from the tomb of A. Julius Pompilius, the Aurelian general—possibly also a trumpet? (Right) a vexillum-type standard, from an Augustan coin reverse.

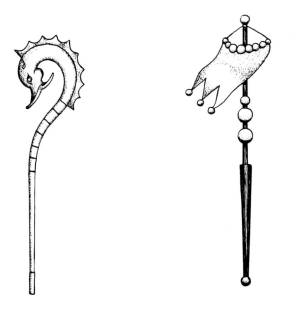

Sarmatians

In the vast Russian steppe, a group of mounted Indo-Europeans, known as Iranians, lived a highly developed nomadic life. They had moved into areas vacated by those Indo-Europeans now living in Europe. Some had invaded India in about B.C. 1200, others had founded the empires of the Medes and Persians. By about the 5th century B.C., those still living on the Eurasian steppe were the Scythians to the west, with Sarmatians to the east of them and Sakas further to the east. Probably as a result of Chinese operations against nomads on their western frontiers, the steppe was set in motion. The Sarmatians moved west and obliterated the Scythians, whose remnants fled to the Danube and Crimea. By the middle of the 2nd century B.C. the Sarmatians became known in Europe as the Iazyges and Roxolani, and those remaining to the east, the Alans. It is believed that Sarmatian success against the Scythians was due to the creation of a force of super-heavy cavalry, both man and horse being completely armoured in some of the formations. These 'cataphracts' operated as a shock force alongside the traditional horse-archer formations used by all mounted nomads.

Neither Thracians nor Sarmatians were Germans. The reasons for their mention in this small work are several. The Dacians were a Thracian people, but Dacia was occupied also by Daco-Germans, and in the north-east by Celto-Dacians. The Sarmatian Roxolani became firm allies of the Dacians, supplying them with the only heavy cavalry force in the Dacian army. With the destruction of Dacia, Rome brought her forces into direct contact with the eastern German tribes, an area which was, in due time, overrun by the German Gepids. In 85 A.D., Dacian forces attacked Roman defences in Moesia, harrying the countryside and killing the Governor. The Emperor Domitian commanded initial operations to clear Moesia of invaders, but later passed control of the operations to Cornelius Fuscus. The campaign was carried into eastern Dacia, but the weight of Dacian numbers gradually drove the Roman forces back, and, in a final battle, they were wiped out, Fuscus suffering the fate of his army. Roman military honour was restored to some degree by the battle of Tapae, in 89 A.D.,

Dacian warriors, 2nd century AD

Marcomanni and Quadi, 1st-2nd centuries AD

C

Gothic warriors, 4th century AD

Gothic warriors, 4th century AD

E

Frankish warriors, 5th century AD

'Anglo-Saxon' warriors, 5th century AD

1

2

3

German soldiers of Roman Army, 4th-5th centuries AD

where the Dacians were thoroughly beaten. Decabalus, the King of Dacia, was forced to pay an annual tribute to Rome and to allow Roman armies passage through Dacian territory. That the Emperor did not recognise the victory as conclusive is borne out by the fact that he refused the title of 'Dacicus' at this juncture.

In 98 A.D., the Emperor Trajan came to power. The situation he inherited was one of increasing unease about the northern frontiers. Rome faced constant threat from German tribes in the west; and the Dacians were expanding their strongholds, it was believed, in readiness for another attack. Dacian culture at this time was far in advance of that of their fellow European barbarians. It was, in all recognisable aspects, an embryo civilization. Towns were beginning to develop from the great defended strongholds called *oppida*, such as the capital at Sarmizegethusa. Centres of importance were defended by minor *oppida* and other outposts. Trade was well organized and encouraged; silver and gold work, pottery, iron implements and weapons, of extremely high quality, were produced for home consumption and export to the sophisticated Roman world in the south. It was this nascent civilization which now attracted increased Roman military interest.

In the winter of 100–101 A.D., Trajan massed ten legions, vexillations of other legions, and huge numbers of auxiliary troops of all kinds at Viminacium, a military base on the south bank of the Danube. The Roman army of conquest crossed the Danube on pontoon bridges, into Dacian territory, in the spring of 101 A.D. No opposition was offered until the army reached the general area of Tapae, where they were confronted by a large Dacian force. The ensuing battle was indecisive. The Dacians retreated to the mountains, killing livestock and burning crops to delay the Roman advance. After a further advance the Roman forces settled into winter quarters. The Dacians, together with their Sarmatian allies, the Roxolani, mounted an attack in Lower Moesia which was repulsed by the Romans. During the winter the Romans occupied themselves with carrying out marvels of engineering.

In the spring of 102 A.D., the Romans attacked Sarmizegethusa through the Red Tower Pass.

During the whole of this period Dacian emissaries were sent to Trajan, who constantly refused them audience. Finally receiving a deputation of prominent nobles, he sent them back with terms which the Dacian king, Decabalus, refused. After a further major battle Decabalus surrendered and Roman forces occupied the Dacian capital, Sarmizegethusa.

By 105 the Dacians had re-armed, taking the Roman garrison commander of Sarmizegethusa hostage; he in turn, took the initiative away from the Dacians by swallowing poison. Once again the Dacians ravaged the Roman province of Moesia. With great effort the Romans relieved the province before winter closed in. In the spring of 106 the Romans mounted a two-pronged assault on Sarmizegethusa, which they put to siege. When all seemed lost, some nobles took poison; others— including Decabalus—escaped. Those who fled were pursued ruthlessly; Decabalus was sur-

Angons—**heavy Germanic javelins with iron heads and shanks; length, including wooden shaft, was probably about 210cm (7ft). Examples from (left to right) France, Germany, Austria and England. The design was, obviously, intended to kill or cripple efficiently; the length of the iron shank suggests that the** *angon* **was used in hand-to-hand combat, where there was a danger of the head being lopped off. The similarity to the classic Roman** *pilum* **raises the question of whether the** *angon* **was also intended to weigh down the enemy's shield when thrown.**

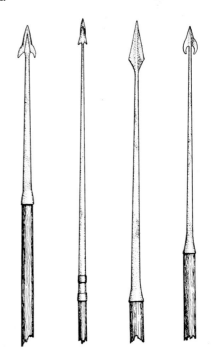

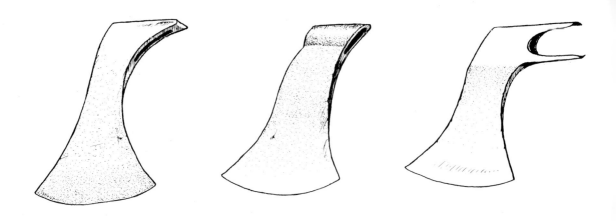

rounded, but, before capture, took his own life by cutting his throat. After the reduction of remaining pockets of resistance, large parts of Dacian territory were annexed as a Roman province.

The Marcomannic Wars

By the middle of the 2nd century, pressure on Rome's northern frontier was mounting as the numerical increase among German tribes impelled their leaders to look for new ground. Goths and other German tribesmen began to move south-east in a steady stream. This movement blossomed into the Gothic nation of southern Russia and the Gepid nation of the Carpathians; the Astingi (Asding) Vandals moved into territory west of the Roman province of Dacia, formerly dominated by the Sarmatian Iazyges. The Roman military command must have followed these developments with foreboding. To the north-west, the Rhine tribes were entering into the super-tribe status of permanent federation. As early as the 1st century A.D. pressure was building on the middle Danube frontier; Roman strongholds had existed with Dacian agreement in the area since the first conquest of Dacia in 106 A.D., on the left banks of the rivers Danube, March and Thaya. During the winter of 166–7, the Lombards, a west German group, crossed the frozen Rhine, carrying with them the Lacringi, Victofali and Ubii. They were immediately followed by a breakthrough of Marcomanni, Quadi and Sarmatian Iazyges in the central Danube area. From then on a kind of 'blitzkrieg', launched by a barbarian conspiracy, sucked in ever-increasing numbers of barbarians,

in spite of a Roman offensive in 170, directed against the Quadi in particular. Roman armies were by-passed on the left and right flanks, and Greece was invaded. Early in 171 Italy too was subjected to brief invasion, which was quickly nullified by Roman forces rushed from the frontier areas. Later in the year Marcus Aurelius rid the Empire of invaders, and peace was negotiated with the Quadi and Iazyges. In 172 the Marcomanni were attacked by Roman forces on the Danube. The Quadi, breaking their treaty with Rome, assisted their Suebian kinsmen. After defeating the Marcomanni, Marcus turned to the Quadi, who were attacked and defeated in 173. The Quadi then made peace. In 174, Roman troops attacked the Iazyges, whereupon the Quadi broke their treaty once more. The war continued into 175, until an armistice was declared in the summer of that year.

During these vicious wars, serious weaknesses in the defences of the north were exposed. The Empire had been invaded and devastated. The constant fighting had made extremely heavy demands on the army at all levels, and, at one point, the gladiatorial schools were emptied in a desperate experiment. The struggle with Rome during the Marcomannic wars had brought far-reaching changes to the Germanic peoples, and created in them an eagerness to launch more assaults on the colossus in the south. Sixteen of Rome's 33 legions manned the northern frontier, together with large numbers of auxiliary troops, at the end of the Marcomannic wars—an end which proved to be only a beginning for the Germans.

The tribes most closely involved in these wars,

the Marcomanni and Quadi, were Germans belonging to the Suebian group of tribes. These Germans had become relatively civilized after a long period of contact with Noricum and Pannonia. Their close knowledge of the operational system and eager acquisition of the technology of the Roman army made these tribes formidable opponents.

The Goths

From their geographical position the Goths, the most powerful Germanic group, seem to have been the last of that family to settle in Europe. They occupied territory in Scandinavia and what is now northern Prussia, under various names given them by classical writers, such as Gothones and Guttones, Gothini and Getae (Gaudae). Their own name for themselves appears to have been the Gutthinda. To return momentarily to the Dacian wars: a strong component of the Dacian army (including the Celtic Bastarnae and the Germans), rather than submit to Trajan, had withdrawn. They had dispersed or been absorbed, probably by other tribes or even by the Goths during their movements south at a later date. From the latter years of the second century A.D., the Goths were in possession of large tracts of country north of the Danube, on the coast of the Euxine as far east as the Tauric Chersonese or Crimea, deep in territory once belonging to the Sarmatian Roxolani, from whom they learned the use of heavy cavalry, the *kontos* (a large, heavy lance), and the stirrup.

These shock troops, heavy cataphract cavalry, were not completely new. Cataphracts had been in existence among Iranian nomads for centuries. The Sarmatians had perfected their use, which had enabled them to defeat the Royal Scythians and move into control of their territory. The Goths seem to have overthrown the Sarmatians by their ferocity in battle, probably hamstringing the horses (a German tactic). Thus, equipped with a heavy cavalry force to support the masses of traditional infantry, they faced the Roman army of the 3rd century, which was now composed largely of Germans, Illyrians and North Africans.

In the mid-3rd century Goths broke into the Balkans, killing the Emperor Decius (Hostilianus). This was followed, in 256, by a cave-in of the Rhine frontier. Gaul was overrun by the Franks and

Reconstruction of a guardsman of the *Germani Corporis Custodes*, **in palace duty dress. These were picked men who formed a personal bodyguard for the emperors from the time of Augustus until about 70 A.D., and again from the early 3rd century onwards. They were often used to counter the ambitions of the Praetorian Guard.**

Alemanni, some of them reaching Spain and Italy. The Goths, after exhausting the Balkans, also spread into Anatolia. Their stay in the Balkans was marked by constant defeats by Roman forces led by the Illyrian Emperors.

In 275 A.D. Rome formally abandoned Dacia, which was promptly occupied by the Gepids and

Two iron *franciscas* **recovered in England. (British Museum)**

the western branch of the numerous Goths, known as the Visigoths. On the Rhine, the angle formed by the Danube in the Black Forest region was also vacated by Rome and occupied by the Alemanni.

Roman troops of the 4th century were finding it no easy matter to defeat a German tribe. Imperial troops lacked the confidence and homogeneity of earlier centuries. Consequently they needed more careful handling in the field. The Germans, by contrast, were organising themselves into super-tribes. New confederacies were now established: the Saxons in the north, Burgundians south of them, Franks north of the Main and the Alemanni to their south. Large formations of the Roman army were made up of Franks, Alemanni, Goths, Vandals, Heruli, Quadi, Marcomanni and Sarmatian Alans. Germans now officered many units, some individuals rising to the highest ranks in the Imperial army. Deserted areas around the frontiers were resettled with ex-prisoners of war from German tribes. More importantly from a military point of view, German tribes were allowed to settle by treaty, under their own chieftains, as 'federates', in return for military service. By way of extension of this policy, clever diplomacy was conducted beyond the frontiers.

Mainly at the expense of Slavonic tribes, the great Gothic leader Ermanarich directed a rapid expansion of his Ostrogoths—the eastern Goths—into the Baltic and across the Don, occupying the little Roman protectorate of the Bosporan kingdom. The assassination of Ermanarich brought distracting confusion to the Ostrogoths at a perilous time. In 370 A.D. rumours were reaching them from their eastern outposts that a people of unusually ugly appearance were moving west across the steppe. Ostrogothic expansion in the east had brought them into contact with true nomadic peoples, Iranians and Finns. In the east they had adopted the nomadic way of life. It was possibly this eastern expansion under Ermanarich which had triggered the avalanche of Huns and Sarmatian Alans, which now headed their way.

The Huns, a Turco-Mongol people, had developed a large, powerful, composite bow, an improved version of the traditional weapon used by the nomadic horse-archer. With this they had been able to penetrate the armour worn by Chinese soldiers, thus nullifying the worst effects of the forward policy of Chinese military authorities, which had set them in motion towards the West. The use of this bow had also been instrumental in their defeat of Iranian nomads, the most westerly of whom were the Alans. Here again, Hunnish arrows were able to penetrate armour worn by Iranian cataphracts. The Huns, however, saw the value of using these large numbers of heavy cavalrymen to subsidise their own small force of armoured horsemen. The Goths who now stood in their path had an army consisting of vast numbers of lightly armed bowmen and cavalry, some of whom would be armed in Sarmatian fashion. The Ostrogothic armies were sent reeling in a south-westerly direction, their empire destroyed. The Visigoths fared no better. The Gepids became Hunnish vassals on the Hungarian steppe. Visigoths, Ostrogoths and Astingi Vandals asked for sanctuary within the Roman Empire, and were allotted territory along the Danube by the Emperor Valens. This immense and voracious host crossed into Roman territory and passed straight into the toils of corrupt prefects and merchants, who

Fourteen spearheads, a sword, three iron bosses and an iron *francisca* **head recovered at Croydon, Surrey. (British Museum)**

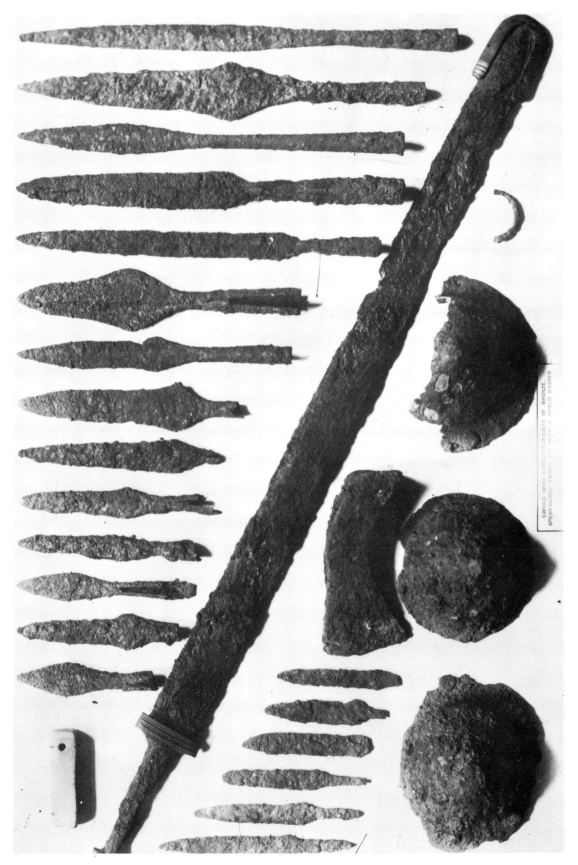

SWORD WITH SCABBARD, 4 BUTTS OF BRONZE,
SPEAR HEADS, KNIFE, AND HEAD & SHIELD BOSSES

disarmed them, and charged exorbitant prices for bad grain and rotting meat. As money ran out, slaves were taken in payment for the dog-meat now offered. Gothic patience ran out and, after breaking into Roman arsenals to regain their weapons, they made alliance with the remaining free Alans and invaded Thrace. They were met at Adrianople by the Emperor Valens and the army of the Eastern Empire.

Visigothic and Ostrogothic infantry were in laager behind their wagons and the Ostrogothic cavalry were in the country foraging when the Romans deployed and began the attack on the laager. At this point, the Ostrogothic cavalry appeared back from foraging and charged the right wing of the Romans, whereupon the Gothic infantry left the laager and attacked and broke the Roman cavalry. The Roman infantry were then

The Roman Empire on the eve of the great Germanic Migrations, in about 395 A.D.

systematically destroyed. When night fell the remnants were able to escape. The catastrophe at Adrianople in 378 A.D. was the worst defeat for the Roman army since Republican times. Among the dead were the Emperor of the Eastern Empire, Valens, the Grand Master of Cavalry, the Grand Master of Infantry, the Count of the Palace, 35 commanders of different corps, and nearly the whole of the Roman army of the east—estimated at 40,000 deaths.

Six years after Adrianople, Goths, Vandals and other Germans, numbering about the same as those lost in the disaster, were enlisted under their own chieftains as cavalrymen in the army of the East.

Meanwhile the Visigoths, frustrated by their inability to take walled towns, were encouraged to quieten down in 382. They became unsettled again in 396, and were persuaded to resettle in north-west Greece. In 402–3 they invaded Italy, only to be promptly defeated by the army of the

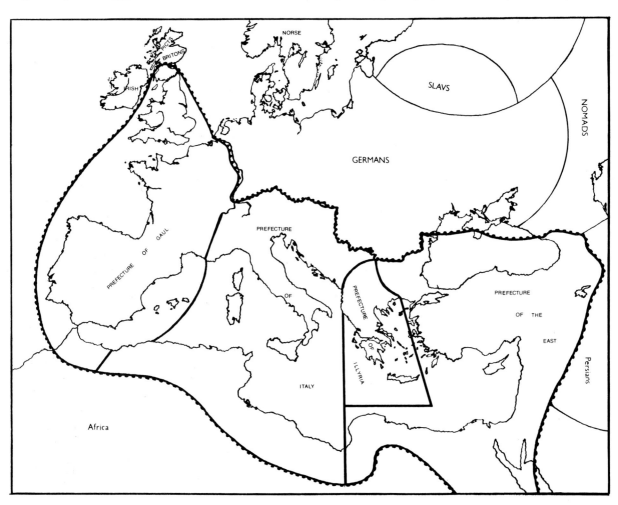

West, commanded by the Romano-Vandal general, Stilicho. In 405 Stilicho defeated a mixed army of Ostrogoths. Quadi and Astingi Vandals with an army which had to be reinforced from units manning the frontier on the Rhine, from Bavaria and Britain. On the last day of 406 another coalition—of Marcomanni, Quadi, Astingi and Siling Vandals—crossed the frozen Rhine into Gaul, accompanied by a clan of dispossessed Sarmatian Alans. Gaul was defenceless and they harried far and wide. After three years they were allowed to cross the Pyrenees into Spain, where they settled on the Atlantic seaboard.

Angles, Saxons and Jutes

German warriors were used extensively in defence of the Empire, and Britain was no exception. Batavian, Frisian, Frankish and Saxon soldiers were used in Britain from the 2nd century, a tradition which the Romano-British continued. In the 3rd and 4th centuries a chain of forts were built around the coastal areas, harried by Saxon raiders, these forts being manned by a special force under the command of the 'Count of the Saxon Shore'. Archaeological evidence from areas previously well populated in north Germany, Denmark and the North Sea coast shows that soon after 400 A.D. an extensive migration had taken place, and continental settlement sites were abandoned. No evidence of villages built after the 4th century exists in some coastal areas. Cremation sites used for 300 years show very limited use; they contain only a few late 5th-century urns. In Danish bogs, votive deposits stop abruptly. In 410 the Saxons attacked Britain in earnest.

At some stage in Saxon involvement with Britain the decision was taken—together with Angles, Frisians, Jutes, and a small number of Franks and Slavonic Wends—to migrate into the rich farmlands of southern Britain. Mercenaries and pirates, fishermen and farmers brought their families over for permanent settlement. Roman troops had been withdrawn to reinforce the Rhine armies fighting desperately to hold the collapsing northern frontier; and the Romanized British were advised, in a letter from the Emperor Honorius, to organize themselves in a programme of self-help, offering freedom to slaves who responded to the call. The Romano-British did indeed organise, in an admirable way, in sharp contrast to the response in Gaul, which was subjugated within 50 years by the Franks. The numbers of barbarians involved may have been greater than those of the Anglo-Saxons, but British resistance was more stubborn. Some Romano-Britons escaped from the south-west,

The hilt of an Anglo-Saxon ring-sword of about the 6th century A.D., found at King's Field, Faversham, Kent. (British Museum)

settling on the Brest Peninsula, where they became known as Bretons. Resistance to the Saxons was so determined in the 6th century that many German migrants returned to their homelands or settled in north-western Gaul, by courtesy of the Franks[1]. In the mid-6th century the Anglo-Saxon advance began again, into Wiltshire and towards the rich prizes of Devon and Somerset, the best farmland in Britain. This was the final phase of the permanent Germanising of a large part of the British mainland. As in other parts of Roman Europe previously, the cities were gradually depopulated until only squatters occupied small precincts. To the German warrior-farmers, cities meant nothing except as places of wonder, built by giants.

Stilicho, the Romano-Vandal, had excited the distrust of the Emperor Honorius because of his vaulting ambition, and was consequently murdered. Once removed, Stilicho could not bargain with the German leaders. Alaric, king of the Visigoths, presented his demands for land subsidies and military command at the gates of Rome. The Roman authorities, now safely resident in Ravenna, refused his requests: this led to an immediate but half-hearted sack of the city. The political effect, however, was devastating. Roman prestige plummeted. The Visigoths marched away to the south with some idea of crossing to North Africa, where they could control Roman corn-lands. In southern Italy, Alaric died, thus enabling undivided Roman attention to be directed northward over the Alps. The Visigoths were finally led out of Italy by Alaric's brother Athaulf, to the Rhineland, where they assisted Roman forces in the pacification of that area. In 414 they trekked into Spain, where, by 416, they had exterminated the Siling Vandals and Alans. The Astingi Vandals and Suebian Germans were saved by Roman intervention. The Visigoths accepted extensive lands in southern Gaul, north of the Pyrenees.

The Empire of Attila

By the 5th century the Huns controlled a vast area of German territory and pasture, once belonging to Iranian nomads, stretching back to the Caspian. In 436 they attacked the Burgundians, who moved into Roman land around Geneva as *foederates* (settled allies).

In 451 Attila led an army composed of Huns, Alans, Goths and other Germans into Gaul. In an inconclusive battle at Campus Mauriacus a mixed army of Romans, Burgundians, Salian Franks and Visigoths checked him. The following year the Huns raided Italy, but were bought off. Attila died in Hungary in 453. After his death the Hunnish Empire split into disunited groups led by the dead Khan's sons. Their German subjects destroyed the Huns in a battle fought at Nedao in Dacia; the remnants were absorbed by the Roman army and by other nomads on the steppe.

While the Romans and other German tribes were occupied with the Huns, the Astingi Vandals invaded North Africa from Spain in 428, where they took over the best provinces and, under King Gaiseric, built a Vandal fleet which turned to piracy. In about 470 the Visigoths descended into Spain, becoming its ruling caste, while still holding territories in Gaul.

De-Germanising the Eastern Army

The Emperor of the East, Zeno (457–474), used Isaurians (semi-civilised Anatolian mountaineers) in the Imperial Guard, and formed new regiments of Isaurians and Armenians. He also induced the Goths remaining in the eastern Empire to migrate to Italy, enabling him to leave his successor an army purged of truculent Germans.

One of the final moves which must be mentioned before closing this survey is that of the Franks, who moved into northern Gaul in 486, expanding into Alemannic and Visigothic territory led by their king, Clovis, who died in 511 A.D.

While the Goths climbed to the zenith of power under their king Theodoric the Great (451–526), the German tribes involved in the great migrations settled down among their Romanised subjects. The last move was made in the 6th century by the Lombards, who, to avoid nomadic pressure, moved west. In 568 they settled in the Po Valley and some lands to the south. The next out-pouring of Germanic peoples began in the 8th century, when they were known as Vikings, Rus, Varangians and Normans.

---

[1] According to the tantalisingly fragmentary accounts, this rolling back of the Germanic invasion was the work of the legendary Arthur.

The Germanic conquest of the Western Roman Empire: Europe in about 476 A.D.

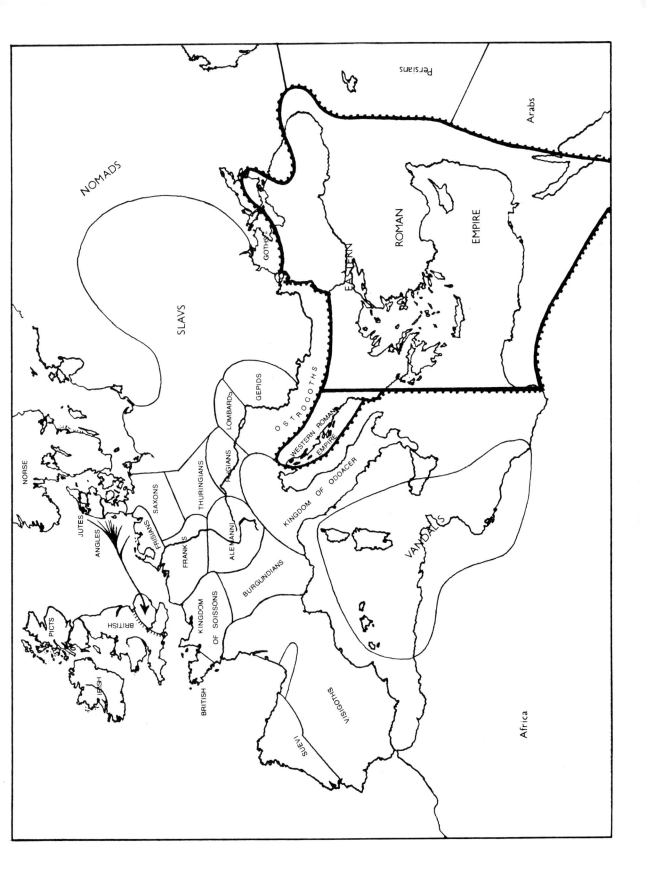

33

The Plates

In spite of 50 years of archaeological activity in the area inhabited by the Germanic tribes, much remains unknown or—inexcusably—unpublished. These colour plates cannot, realistically, be considered in the same light as paintings depicting later periods for which we have generous pictorial references. The surviving artefacts, and genuinely contemporary pictorial sources such as Roman triumphal sculpture, are too few; their interpretation into an integrated overall scheme is too problematical. Nevertheless, as the body of the text has shown, we *do* have more evidence than might be supposed. We believe that these plates—based upon the careful sketches prepared by the author in the course of extensive research—achieve a reasonable reconstruction of the appearance and character of these magnificent 'barbarians'.

One general thought should perhaps be recorded. In discussing the clothing of this period one often encounters phrases such as 'coarsely woven' or 'roughly made'—and these may be seriously misleading. Certainly, Roman writers make a point of the material poverty of some German tribes; but the subject and the time-scale are vast, and it is dangerous to generalise from the particular. We should be on guard against that general historical prejudice which inclines us to think of earlier peoples as, by definition, 'cruder' than ourselves. Their surviving artefacts completely disprove this, time and time again. In societies whose every need was supplied by skilled handicrafts, a mastery of tools, materials and techniques was often allied with a highly artistic instinct. The surviving Celtic weapons and armour from early in our period were made by smiths who had nothing whatever to learn from us; why should not the same be true of their womenfolk, who doubtless passed the skills of spinning and weaving down from mother to daughter as an important element in their social rôle? Why should we assume, in our bottomless arrogance, that the peoples of Iron Age Europe were any less competent at the daily tasks of their world than we are at ours?

A few precious finds of fabric clothing preserved in northern bogs suggest sturdy, long-wearing materials, sometimes with animal hair woven into the textile for added strength; but though 'coarse' in the sense of 'hairy', these fragments are by no means crudely made. The cloth is of a range of weights roughly comparable to, say, a light modern overcoat, or a heavy tweed. (It is interesting to note that modern experiments show the wool of undernourished highland sheep to be *finer* than that of fattened lowland flocks.) We have evidence of simple but pleasing decorative borders. The written descriptions of checkered patterns and stripes are supported by surviving examples of small, complex, neatly-worked 'tartans'. One such is the woman's robe from Huldre Fen, and the associated scarf; the robe is cut to fall in generous and graceful folds, and is finely sewn. The vegetable dyes used at this time probably gave quite bright colours when new, fading gradually with age into a subtle range of muted shades.

While the materials and workmanship of clothing, armour and weapons doubtless varied from region to region and from generation to generation, we should also remember that there were no rigid cultural frontiers in those days. The borders of the Empire were flexible, and porous; and a considerable trade between the Mediterranean world and the unpacified north and east of Europe continued throughout our period. Once the great migrations got under way, the mixture of styles to be seen in any one area or among any one tribal confederation must presumably have grown even more liberal.

A: Early German warriors, 1st century B.C.–1st century A.D.

The rider **A1** is mounted on a tough but probably poor-quality pony; we may infer this from the fact that the Romans, who used horsemen like this extensively, gave them better horses before training them to operate in formation. His harness is rudimentary, with few metal fittings; the 'saddle' is a folded blanket held by a sturdy leather cinch. His fringed cloak, tunic and long trousers, tied at the ankle, are all of wool. His shield is of wood covered with leather, with thin bronze edging and an iron boss, held by a central grip across the inside of the boss. Armament is limited to a light spear—*framea*—two shorter javelins, and a bronze belt-knife.

A2 and **A3** belong to one of the extensive group of Suebic tribes; their hair is dressed in the style known as the 'Suebian knot', which involved either drawing it up into a top-knot, or drawing it over to the right and knotting it above the temple. **A2** has a Celtic-type shield, whose metal boss was used offensively in combat. He is armed with a late Celtic sword of La Tène design, and a dagger; in battle he would carry several javelins, as does **A3**. This younger warrior, dressed only in a breech-clout of natural wool, carries an oval Celtic shield with a prominent central rib swelling into a boss; he might be armed with a knife in addition to his javelins.

B: Dacians, 2nd century A.D.
The chieftain, **B1**, wears a bronze helmet of Phrygian type, a corselet of iron 'leaf'-scale armour, and a black wool tunic and trousers decorated with red and white embroidery at hems and lower legs. The wool cloak, in a simple 'tartan' pattern, would probably be discarded before battle; plain colours, or a 'herringbone tweed' texture are also possible. Dacian shields shown on Trajan's Column are oval in shape, and those sculpted on the base of the column show how large and how richly decorated they were. A shield found at Pietra-Rosie in Romania, at present unpublished, bears plant motifs, and the likeness of a boar in the centre. Varieties of Dacian shields may be present on the triumphal relief from Trajan's Forum, now to be seen on the Arch of Constantine: one borne by a dismounted Praetorian trooper is oblong, with floral decoration, and a hexagonal type decorated with four Celtic carnyx trumpets and torques is seen carried by a Dacian.

The dismounted Dacian horseman, **B2**, wears a fringed cloak held by a silver ring-brooch, and natural-coloured linen tunic and trousers decorated at hem, cuffs and lower leg with red and black embroidery. His weapons are a seven-foot spear, and a long bronze La Tène sword supported by a waist belt with added bronze plates: such weapons were probably still being produced in eastern Europe by Celtic smiths. His horse would be of better quality than the pony of figure **A1**.

Two iron spearheads and an *angon*-head, found at Astwick, Bedfordshire. (British Museum)

The Dacian tribal warrior, **B3**, wears cream-coloured trousers, sometimes decorated with bands of black embroidered patterns. The two-handed weapon is the murderous *falx*, an iron battle-scythe with the cutting edge on the inside of the curve; the *falx*, and the similar but one-handed *sica*, were the ethnic weapons of the Thracian peoples in general, and were used by part of the infantry of all Thracian groups.

C: The Marcomanni and Quadi, 1st–2nd centuries A.D.
These figures represent the most politically advanced and cohesive group of Germanic tribes of the 1st and 2nd centuries A.D. They lived in close contact with the Roman Empire and were, in consequence, exposed to strong Mediterranean influences. The chieftain, **C2**, wears a bronze helmet which appears in reasonable detail on the sculpted sarcophagus of a late Antonine general now in the Museo Nazionale delle Terme, Rome. We show it here as a Roman cavalry battle helmet mounted with a fabulous beast head to suit

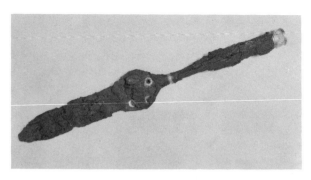

A richly-decorated iron spearhead with bronze inlay, recovered at Great Chesterfield. (British Museum)

barbarian taste; it may, in fact, have been a cavalry sports helmet of a pattern normally equipped with a trilobate face mask, which has been removed. His mail corselet is of iron, and may have been of native manufacture; the possibility of continuing manufacture of weaponry by Celtic craftsmen in the *barbaricum* is a distinct and attractive one. The oval shield has an indent top and bottom; this pattern, and a dilobate type, seem to be peculiar to these Suebian Germans, but they also used the more common hexagonal and round patterns. The sword is of Roman origin, and has an eagle-headed pommel—there was a considerable trade in Empire-made weapons across the frontiers.

The upper-class warrior, **C3**, wears two woollen tunics, and the usual long trousers. The short sleeves of the outer tunic may have been 'notched' part way up from the hem, centrally: this feature is seen in sculptures on the sarcophagus of a Roman general who fought these tribes on the middle Danube. The hair is arranged in the 'Suebian knot', drawn over to the right temple. His weapons are a native sword on a leather baldric, and a battle-axe. Both **C2** and **C3** would have fought either mounted or on foot, as circumstances dictated. **C1** is an ordinary Suebian tribal warrior, dressed in rough woollen material with a warm jerkin of fur or fleece. He carries a javelin, a *sax*, and a shield of an old pattern, and wears amber and meerschaum beads in a double row at the neck. The cross-gartering on the legs cannot be absolutely dated to this early period; but several well-preserved corpses dating from the Celtic and Roman Iron Ages, recovered from northern European bogs, appear to wear this style—e.g. the Rendswühren Fen find of 1871. The fur shoes are

taken from a find in Fraeer Fen, Jutland—they were made of two thicknesses, the fur on the inside of the inner layer and the outside of the outer layer. In the background is a *draco* standard, a hollow bronze beast head with an attached 'wind-sock' of coloured fabric.

D: Gothic heavy cavalryman and infantryman, 4th century A.D.

In battle the horseman, **D1**, would have carried a long spear and a number of shorter javelins in addition to his long, 'Sarmatian' sword. His helmet, of late Roman cavalry type, is of iron with copper-gilt skinning; his mail corselet is of gilded iron, and his cloak is fastened with an iron and gilt bow-brooch. The hems and cuffs of clothing were often decorated with fur trim or embroidery; linen tunics were sometimes patterned on upper arm, neck and skirt. The round, slightly concave shield has a Roman iron boss. His mount, of about 16 hands, has iron and bronze harness fittings, and the saddle-arches are covered with stamped bronze plates, found in many Gothic burials. The infantryman, **D2**, wears two tunics, the upper one trimmed with fur; embroidery or applied cloth shapes may sometimes have been seen, in bands, simple geometric motifs, or 'dagging', to judge from Roman miniatures of the period which are thought to show Gothic influence. Shields also bore geometric shapes in primary colours. (Note that on this and some other plates we have deliberately brought such items as swords around to a slightly unconvincing angle in order to allow more visible detail.)

E: Gothic types, 4th century A.D.

The foot-soldiers, **E1** and **E3**, wear a variety of styles of woollen and linen clothing. Some probably wore tunics richly bordered with brocade or fur. This nomadic warrior people overran enemies of many groups—Slavonic, Sarmatian, Roman—and may be presumed to have profited by their success. Some tattooing of face, arms and chest is possible. Weapons ranged from bunches of javelins, and longer spears, through *saxes*, long swords and battleaxes, to bows. The bow illustrated is about 168cm long, with bronze 'nocks'; the arrows were about 90cm long, and some were tipped with armour-piercing piles. Shields were round or oval, with iron bosses, and some probably bore geometric patterns. The unarmoured trooper, **E2**, carries a spear and a number of javelins and a long single-edged sword. Roman miniatures of the period suggest the 'dagged' tunic decoration. The oval shield, about 2ft 6ins by 3ft long, has a central arm-loop and a grip near the rim. Note particularly the wooden stirrups.

F: Frankish warriors, 5th century A.D.
Weapons particularly associated with the Franks were a javelin with a long iron shank, called an *angon* and probably derived from the Roman *pilum*; and the throwing-axe—*francisca*—with a sharply swept head. The shields have prominent bosses, either pointed, domed, or domed with a central 'button'. Note the characteristic hairstyle, with side-braids, top-knot, and the rear of the skull shaved. The writings of Sidonius Apollinaris, a 5th-century Gallo-Roman eyewitness to the Frankish invasion of Gaul, mention tunics dyed and striped in bright colours, and fur belts with inset bosses. He also mentions green cloaks bordered in red; but the scarcity of brooches in grave-finds might suggest that cloaks were not very common. Franks and Gauls enjoyed close contact for some time prior to the 5th century invasions, and it is believed that Franks would have displayed some Gallic influence in their clothing.

G: 'Anglo-Saxons', 5th century A.D.
The so-called 'Anglo-Saxon' raiders and invaders of Britain in the 4th and 5th centuries were not all Angles, Saxons and Jutes. The incoming western Germans were also represented by Frisians, Franks, and probably Alemanni; there were also a number of Wends, a Slavonic people. These figures are representative of three social divisions which were evident even as early as the writings of Tacitus in the 1st/2nd centuries. The chieftain, **G1**, is shown wearing a helmet from a later period of Saxon history—the Benty Grange find, dated to the 7th century, 200 years after the settlement of eastern Britain. It is based upon the so-called *spangenhelm*, however, and this type of composite construction was used in Europe from the 3rd right up to the 12th century, so its appearance here is not anomalous. Its iron frame originally

enclosed some kind of padded cap. The gaps in the frame are filled in with plates of split horn, giving a milky greenish-grey appearance; the helmet is held together with horn-and-hoof glue, and silver rivets in a disc-and-double-axe shape. A small silver cross or 'Thor's hammer' is mounted on the noseguard; and just forward of the apex of the skull is a small boar, decorated with four rows of gold beads and with a silver 'spat' on each quarter, mounted on a curved plate and riveted to the central iron band. The mail shirt is shown with traces of rust after a voyage—the chief's slave would doubtless spend many hours polishing it and greasing it with animal fat! The richly-decorated sword hangs from a baldric fastened by an ornate bronze buckle; in battle the warrior would also carry spears. The conical boss of the buckler was used offensively. The woollen clothing was often decorated at hem and cuffs.

The better-equipped warrior, **G2**, is a member of the chieftain's war-band. Apart from his *angon* he would carry a *francisca* and a short, single-edged sword or long knife—the *sax*. His large oval shield has a bun-shaped iron boss. He wears a 'Thor's hammer' charm on a neck-thong; and his clothing is of better quality than that of **G2**, who is an ordinary warrior/farmer, dressed in simple homespun woollens. He would normally enter battle armed with a spear as well as this one-handed battleaxe, and with a belt-knife.

H: German soldiers of the Imperial Roman Army,
  4th–5th centuries A.D.
H1 and **H3** are representative of the élite German regiments known as *Auxilia Palatina* (Palace Auxiliaries), raised by Constantine the Great; **H2** is a guardsman of the Emperor's German bodyguard—*Germani Corporis Custodes*—and is dressed for palace duty. In general clothing of the period seems to have been well decorated; civilian fashion inside the Empire had followed the barbarian taste for decorative embroidery and appliqué-work, and evidence for highly decorative military clothing may be found on late Roman mosaics, bas-reliefs, plates and manuscripts. Leather belts with ornate iron fittings support long swords which invite comparison with both ancient Celtic styles and with the Roman cavalry *spatha*—with the decline in the

importance of infantry, the old legionary *gladius* had apparently given place to this type of weapon. The large oval shields seem sometimes to have had short, flighted javelins about 30cm long, with an oval lead weight on the shaft, clipped to the inner surface in some way.

Glossary

Alemanni	A confederation of German tribes who settled in Gaul.
Alans	Sarmatian nomads of south-eastern Russia.
Angles	Germans of the Baltic who took part in the settlement of the lowlands of the British mainland.
Angon	A heavy Germanic javelin.
Britons	The collective name for most of the Celts of the British mainland, some of whom settled in Gaul.
Burgundians	Germans of the middle Rhine who settled in Gaul.
Celts	A large group of Indo-Europeans.
Cimbri	A Celtic people of the middle Danube; they are believed by some scholars to be Germans.
Dacians	A Thracian people of eastern Europe, destroyed by Rome.
Foederates	Barbarians allied to Rome by treaty (*foedus*).
Francisca	The German throwing-axe used extensively by the Frankish tribes.
Franks	Germans of the Rhine who expanded into Belgium and eventually most of Gaul.
Frisians	Germans of the coastal lowlands of western Europe, some of whom took part in the settlement of Britain.
Gauls	The continental Celts.
Gepids	German people of the middle Danube; they were absorbed by the Avars, a Turco-Mongol people.
Germans	A large group of Indo-Europeans.
Goths	The most powerful group of ancient Germans. From the Baltic they spread into western Russia, eventually controlling a large part of Gaul, Italy and Spain.
Halstatt	The first Celtic Iron Age, beginning about B.C. 600.
Huns	Turco-Mongol nomads of the Eurasian plains.
Indo-Europeans	Nordic nomads of the Eurasian plains.
Iranians	A large group of Indo-European nomads.
Jutes	German people of the Baltic, who took part in the settlement of lowland Britain.

Iron Anglo-Saxon sword of the 5th to 8th century A.D. (British Museum)

La Tène	The final phase of the Celtic Iron Age beginning about B.C. 350.
Lombards	Germanic people of northern Germany who settled in Italy.
Marcomanni	Germans of the Danube.
Ostrogoths	The eastern branch of the Gothic nation.
Phrygians	A Thracian people of Asia Minor.
Quadi	A German people of the middle Danube.
Salian Franks	Franks of the coast of north-west Europe. 'Salty' Franks.
Sarmatians	Iranian mounted nomads.
Sax (Saex)	Single-edged knives common in the graves of Saxons in Britain and continental Germans.
Saxons	Germans of the Baltic.
Scythians	Iranian horse nomads.
Slavs	A large group of Indo-Europeans.
Suebi	A large group of German tribes.
Spangenhelm	A helmet of composite construction, introduced in Europe during the 3rd century A.D.
Teutons	A modern name for Germanic people.
Teutones	A Celtic tribe, believed by some scholars to be Germans.
Thracians	A large group of Indo-Europeans.
Vandals	Germans of the Baltic who settled in Gaul, Spain and North Africa.
Visigoths	The western branch of the Gothic people, who annexed Spain.
Wends	A Germanized Slavonic people who took part in the German colonization of lowland Britain.

Sources:

The plaster cast copy of Trajan's Column in the Victoria and Albert Museum, Kensington.

Trajan's Column and the Dacian Wars, Lino Rossi

The Arms and Armour of Imperial Rome, H. Russell Robinson

Oriental Armour, H. Russell Robinson

Romania, Dimitru Berciu

For those interested in further reading some books available on the subjects are listed below:

Germania, Tacitus

The Annals of Imperial Rome, Tacitus

The Histories, Tacitus

The Celts, T. G. E. Powell

The Decline and Fall of the Roman Empire, Edward Gibbon

A Study of History, Arnold Toynbee

The World of the Huns, Otto Maenchen-Halfen

The Treasure of Sutton Hoo, Bernice Groskopf

The Age of Arthur, John Morris

The Anglo-Saxons, D. J. V. Fisher

Anglo-Saxon England, Sir Frank Stenton

Roman Britain and the English Settlements, R. G. Collingswood & J. N. L. Myers

Arthur's Britain, L. Alcock

Races of Europe, by Carleton S. Coon

The World of Late Antiquity, P. Brown

The Kingdom of the Franks, P. Lasko

The Barbarian West, J. M. Wallace-Hadrill

The Northern Barbarians, M. Todd

The Penguin Atlas of Ancient History, Colin McEvedy

The Penguin Atlas of Medieval History, Colin McEvedy

Archaeology of Weapons, Ewart Oakeshott

Dark Age Warrior, Ewart Oakeshott

The Dark Ages, edited by David Talbot Rice

The Goths in Spain, E. A. Thompson

Barbarian Europe, Philip Dixon

The Art of War in the Middle Ages, Sir Charles Oman

The Bog People, P. V. Glob

The Vikings and Their Origins, D. Wilson

The Slavs, M. Gimbutas

The Armies and Enemies of Imperial Rome, Phil Barker

Armies of the Dark Ages 600–1066, Ian Heath

Two ring-swords from Faversham, Kent. (British Museum)

Notes sur les planches en couleur

A1 monte un poney rustre mais résistant; il est vêtu de laine et son bouclier a une simple poignée au centre arrière; une lance, *framea*; deux courts javelots et une dague en bronze à la ceinture. **A2, A3** Le style de coiffure Suève consistait à nouer les cheveux soit au sommet de la tête soit sur la tempe. Les boucliers sont une variante du bouclier celtique. Le guerrier plus âgé a une épée du type La Tène et le plus jeune seulement des javelots.

B1 Ce chef porte un casque de style phrygien, une armure de poitrine en écailles et des vêtements de style typiquement Dacien. Notez la décoration sophistiquée du bouclier, transcrite d'après des documents archéologiques et des sculptures. **B2** est un cavalier démonté avec une lance de plus de deux mètres de long et une épée de style La Tène. **B3**, homme d'une tribu avec une redoutable *falx* ou faux de combat Dacienne.

Les Allemands les plus évolués, qui furent le plus longtemps en contact avec la civilisation romaine; le chef, **C2**, porte une version modifiée du casque de cavalerie romain, auquel est ajouté un emblème-animal de crête, et il porte une épée romaine. **C3** est un guerrier de range élevé, en tenue d'hiver – notez les deux tuniques portées ensemble. **C1** est un guerrier plus démuni. Le style des vêtements de ces hommes sont représentés d'après un nombre limité de sculptures ainsi que des corps assez bien préservés, découverts dans des tourbières européennes.

D1 irait au combat avec une longue lance, une brassée de javelots et sa longue épée *sarmatienne*. Ce cavalier aisé a des décorations de cuivre argenté sur son casque et son armure de poitrine. Comme **D2**, il porte des vêtements bordés de fourrure. On en trouve la preuve, ainsi que des motifs brodés géometriques à l'ourlet et aux manchettes, dans des peintures romaines de l'époque; on pense qu'elles sont influencées par le style goth. **D2** est un fantassin; les motifs géometriques simples des boucliers rappellent ceux des troupes romaines de l'époque.

E Types de Goths; ayant conquis de nombreuses tribus slaves et thraces, cette ethnie nomade porte des vêtements et des armes probablement influencés par des courants très divers. L'arc a à peu près 1.68m de long, et les flèches à peu près 90cm; certaines avaient des pointes spéciales pour percer les armures. La décoration de la tunique de ce cavalier est tirée de miniatures romaines. Son bouclier a une boucle pour passer le bras et une poignée près du bord. Notez en particulier ses étriers de bois.

F Notez les armes plus particulièrement attribuées aux Francs—le long javelot, *angon*, et la hache de lancer à deux lames, la francisque. Les coiffures sont caracté-ristiques. Ces costumes sont illustrés d'après des descriptions de Sidonius Apollinaris, un témoin contemporain des Francs.

G1, un chef de tribu. Il porte un casque dont le modèle est basé sur celui trouvé à Benty Grange, d'époque plus tardive que celle-ci, mais dont le modèle s'est étendu sur plusieurs siècles. **G2** fait partie du groupe d'hommes combattant aux côtés du chef; les deux guerriers iraient au combat avec plusieurs javelots en plus de leurs autres armes. Notez l'amulette de Thor autour du cou. **G3**, un simple guerrier-paysan, est moins richement vêtu et équipé.

H1 et **H3** appartiennent aux unités d'élite allemandes—les *Auxilia Palatina*—de l'armée romaine du temps de Constantin et plus tard. **H2** fait partie du corps de garde allemand de l'empereur, le *Germani Corporis Custodes* et il est habillé pour ses fonctions au palais. L'influence croissante des barbares au cours des derniers temps de la période impériale romaine se retrouve dans les costumes aux décorations colorées, dont on trouve de nombreux exemples dans les mosaïques et les peintures de l'époque.

Farbtafeln

A1 reitet ein zähes, jedoch schwächlich gezüchtetes Pony; ganz in Wolle gekleidet, trägt er ein Schutzschild mit einem einzigen Handgriff hinter dem Mittelknopf; ein 'framea' Speer; zwei kurze Wurfspiesse und ein bronzenes Gürtelmesser. **A2, A3** Der schwäbische Haarstil schloss das Knoten des Haares entweder am Oberkopf oder an der rechten Schläfe mit ein. Die Schutzschilde zeigen Variationen der keltischen Stilarten. Der ältere Krieger hat ein Schwert des La Tene Typs, der jüngere nur eine Anzahl von Wurfspiessen.

B1 Dieser Anführer hat einen Helm des phrygischeln Typs, ein Schuppenpanzerbrustschild und Kleidung nach typischem dacianischem Stil. Bemerke, die reiche Verzierung des Schildes, skulpturellem und archeologischem Beweismaterial entnommen. **B2** ist ein abgesessener Kavallerist mit einem sieben Fuss langem Speer und einem La Tene Schwert. **B3**, ein einfacher Stammesmann, hat die tötliche 'falx' oder dacinische Kampfsense.

Der fortgeschrittenste deutsche Volksstamm, der den längsten Kontakt mit Rom hatte; der Stammesführer, **C2**, trägt einen modifizierten römischen Kavalleeriehelm mit zugefügter Spitze in Form eines Biestkopfes, und ein römisches Schwert. **C3** ist ein Krieger der gehobenen Klasse in Winterkleidung —bemerke die zwei zusammengetragenen Tuniken; **C1** ist ein ärmerer Krieger. Der Kleiderschnitt ist in allen Fällen begrenztem skupturellem Beweismaterial sowie von Funden erhaltener Körper in europäischen Sumpflandschaften entnommen.

D1 würde sowohl einen langen Speer als auch ein Bündel Wurfspiesse sowie sein langes 'Sarmatian' Schwert im Kampf tragen. Dieser wohlhabende Reiter hat kupfervergoldete Verzierungen an seinem Helm und Brustschild. Er und **D2** haben beide pelzbesetzte Kleidungsstücke; die römischen Gemälde, von denen man glaubt, dass sie gotischen Einfluss zeigen, dienen uns als Beweismaterial dafür und für Muster einfacher geometrischer Stickerei an Säumen und Ärmelaufschlägen. **D2** ist ein Fusssoldat; der Gebrauch einfacher geometrischer Muster auf dem Schild erinnert an römische Truppen dieser Periode.

E Gotische Typen; diese nomadische Rasse, die viele slavische und thracianische Völker überrannte, mag Einflüsse von einem weiten Gebiet in ihrer Kleidung und Kriegsausrüstung gezeigt haben. Der gezeigte Bogen ist ca. 168cm lang; die Pfeile ca. 90cm, und einige hatten spezielle Spitzen um die Rüstung durchdringen zu können. Die Verzierung der Tunika des Reiters ist von römischen Miniaturen vorgeschlagen. Sein Schild hat eine mittlere Armschleife und einen Handgriff in der Nähe des Randes. Bemerke besonders seine hölzernen Steigbügel.

F Bemerke die Waffen, die besonders mit den Franken in Zusammenhang gebracht werden—den langen 'angon' Wurfspiess und die 'francisca' Wurfaxt. Bemerke die charakteristischen Haarstile. Wir entnehmen die Kostume den Beschreibungen von Sidonius Apollinaris, einem zeitgenössischen Beobachter.

G1, ein Stammesoberhaupt, trägt einen Helm, der auf dem bei Benty Grange gefundenen basiert ist—später als unsere Periode, jedoch von einem Typ, der über verschiedene Jahrhunderte hinweg gesehen wurde. **G2** ist ein Mitglied der Kriegsbande des Führers; im Kampf wurden beide Männer sowohl etliche Wurfspiesse als auch ihre Handwaffen tragen. Bemerke den Thor's Hammer Halsglücksbringer. **G2**, ein einfacher Bauernkrieger, ist nicht so reich gekleidet und ausgerüstet.

H1 und **H3** sind Männer der deutschen Eliteeinheiten—Auxilia Palatina— in der römischen Armee von Konstantin und späteren Kaisern; **H2** ist ein Gardist des Kaisers deutsche Leibwache, 'Germani Corporis Custodes', angezogen für den Palastwachendienst. Der wachsende barbarische Einfluss in der späteren kaiserlichen Zeit ist in den lebhaft verzierten Kostümen zu sehen, für welche wir gutes Beweismaterial in form von Gemälden und Mosaiken dieser Periode haben.